WRITING FOR TODAY

A Course in Improved Writing Skills

Alexandra Swann

Frontier 2000 Media Group, Inc.

Media Group Inc.

Published in the USA by Frontier 2000 Media Group Inc., El Paso, Texas.
ISBN-13: 978-1466236226
ISBN-10: 1466236221

How to Use this Course

Your manuscript is both good and original, but the part that is good is not original, and the part that is original is not good."

SAMUEL JOHNSON

Too often the inexperienced writer finds his work could be accurately described in Johnson's words. In an attempt to write creatively, he ignores the elements of proper grammar and punctuation that make writing lucid and correct. Likewise, when he concentrates on the elements of grammar, punctuation and word usage, the writer often finds it difficult to express himself creatively.

This course will help you learn to write creatively and correctly—to produce work that is both original and good. Grammar and punctuation exercises designed to help you become comfortable with proper English usage are interwoven with creative writing assignments which will help you develop your imagination and your writing style. Unit One examines the parts of speech and then progresses to seven different sentence patterns. Unit Two explores descriptive writing while Unit Three examines narrative writing. Unit Four is devoted to comparison and contrast writing and cause and effect relationships, and Unit Five teaches the art of persuasive writing. Finally, Unit Six examines letter writing, writing in the digital era of emails, blogs and social networking sites, and personal and argumentative essays. A glossary of the parts of speech and sentence parts appears at the beginning of the first unit.

This course has been designed specifically for the independent study student. The material contained in these pages is drawn from the author's experiences teaching writing to students in the community college setting. In preparing this course, I took into consideration the needs of the hundreds of students I taught over a period of several years and designed a course to benefit both the fairly experienced writer and the individual with very little previous writing experience. *Writing for Today* is not a grammar course, however, and it should not be used as a substitute for a good basic course in English grammar. Rather, the grammar and punctuation exercises are included as a handy reference guide for the beginning writer or as a refresher for the writer who may have forgotten some of this material during years spent out of school. Used alone or in conjunction with a basic course in English grammar, *Writing for Today* will serve to reinforce grammatical concepts and provide food for thought that is appetizing.

Because each lesson builds on a preceding one, it is important to complete the assignments in the order in which they appear in the book. All of the lessons have purposely been made short in order to give you the opportunity to thoroughly absorb the material before moving on. Read each lesson carefully, and after mastering the information, complete the review at the end of the lesson and proceed to the next one.

Each unit has its own unit test. The answers to the self-check tests and the unit tests appear in the answer key in the back the course. If a practice or an exercise does not have answers provided for it, this fact will be noted next to the page number in the answer key. If you have missed no more than two of the questions in the self-check tests or unit tests, you are performing well. If you miss three or more questions, do not go forward. Take time to review the material to make sure that you really understand it. When you have finished your review, take the test again and then proceed to the other lessons.

Good luck as you begin your study.

ACKNOWLEDGEMENTS

Excerpts from *The McAloons: A Horse Called Lightning & A House of Clowns* used by permission of Frontier 2000 Media Group Inc. Copyright 2011 by Joyce Swann. All rights reserved.

Knowledge is the foundation and source of good writing.

HORACE, *DE ARTE POETICA* (20 B.C.)

UNIT ONE

Mastering the Basics

THE ENGLISH LANGUAGE AT A GLANCE

PARTS OF SPEECH

Nouns:

Words that name persons, places, things, or ideas. Nouns are often preceded by noun markers; words such as *a, an*, and *the* which tell us that a noun will soon follow.

Pronouns:

Words that take the place of nouns in sentences. Among the most common types of pronouns are personal pronouns which are used to refer to specific people or things who have already been mentioned by the writer.

Verbs:

Words which express action or existence in time (being). Verbs tell us what is being done to the nouns in the sentence, or what the nouns are doing, or what they are.

Adjectives:

Words which modify, or describe, nouns. Adjectives answer questions such as *What Kind*? or *Which one*?

Connectives:

Words which link other words, groups of words, or clauses. Connectives include *coordinating, adverbial, subordinating, relative pronouns* and *special connectives.*

Prepositions:

Words showing relationships between nouns and the sentence. A *prepositional phrase* begins with a *preposition* and usually ends with a *noun* or *pronoun.*

THE ENGLISH LANGUAGE AT A GLANCE

BASIC SENTENCE PARTS

Subject:

The first of two parts of the simple sentence. The *simple subject* is the word which is performing or receiving action in the sentence. The *complete subject* contains the subject and any modifiers.

Predicate:

The second of two parts of the simple sentence. The *simple predicate* is the verb or verb phrase. The *complete predicate* is made up of the *simple predicate* and any words that modify it or complete its meaning.

Complements:

Nouns or adjectives which are part of the predicate and complete a statement made about the subject.

Modifiers:

Words that describe or add to the meaning of one of the sentence parts.

Phrases:

Groups of words that act as one grammatical unit. Types of phrases include: *appositive, prepositional* and *verbal.*

Clauses:

Groups of words in the sentences which contain their own subjects and predicates. Clauses may be *independent*—they express a complete thought and could constitute a sentence on their own—or they may be *dependent*—they rely on the rest of the sentence to complete their thought.

LESSON ONE: NOUNS

By the time you have completed this lesson, you should be able to do the following:

- Identify nouns.
- Distinguish between common and proper nouns.
- Distinguish between concrete and abstract nouns.

A *noun* is a word which names a *person, place, thing*, or *idea. Singular* nouns name *one* person, place, thing, or idea; *plural* nouns name *more than one.* Nouns generally form their plurals by adding *s* or *es* to the end of the singular form of the word.

Concrete nouns name people, places, or things which we can *touch, see, smell,* or *otherwise experience through our senses*. The following words are examples of concrete nouns: *cow, horse, fence, brick, man, woman, child, house, grass, trees.*

Abstract nouns name *ideas, qualities,* or *characteristics* which we cannot see or touch. These nouns name emotions and feelings. The following words are examples of abstract nouns: *love, joy, peace, hatred, anger, friendship, sadness, exhaustion.*

Common nouns are *general words* which name *people, places, things,* or *ideas.* They do not specify any particular person, place or thing; they are used when we want to discuss people or things in general. Common nouns are not capitalized unless they appear at the beginning of a sentence. The following words are examples of common nouns: *bridge, bank, country, state, man, woman, dog.* Often common nouns are preceded by noun markers: words such as *a, an*, and *the.* These words often tell us that a noun will soon follow.

Proper nouns name *specific people, places,* or *things*. Proper nouns are capitalized regardless of their location in the sentence. Look at the following examples of proper nouns and compare this list with the list of common nouns above: *Brooklyn Bridge, Citibank, France, Oregon, Fred Smith, Jeanne Davis, Lassie.* Notice that the words above refer to *one specific bridge, bank, country, state, man, woman,* and *dog.*

Collective nouns name *groups of people or things*. Words such as *police, committee, military, navy, team, faculty, personnel,* and *management,* are all collective nouns.

Collective nouns are considered *singular* when the noun is referred to as a unit but *plural* when we are referring to the individual members of the noun. Look at the following examples:

> The faculty *has* voted *itself* a pay raise. (The unit has voted for the raise.)

> The faculty *were* pleased with the outcome. (The individual members were pleased.)

PRACTICE

Now that you have completed the first lesson, go back to the beginning and review the objectives for this lesson. On a piece of notepaper, in one sentence each, define common nouns, proper nouns, abstract nouns, concrete nouns, and collective nouns. When you have completed your definitions, look through the lesson to see if you have written correct definitions for each of these. Then complete the self-check test below:

Self-Check Test

Exercise A:

Identify each of the following nouns as concrete or abstract by putting a C next to each concrete noun and an A next to each abstract noun. Check your answers with the answer key in the back of the book:

1. love
2. joy
3. farm
4. patience
5. hill
6. man
7. woman
8. anger

9. grass
10. rocks

11. cat
12. hatred

13. fear
14. life

Exercise B:

Identify the following nouns as being common or proper by marking a C next to each common noun and a P next to each proper noun. Check your answers with the answer key:

1. Fred
2. man

3. child
4. Billy

5. New York
6. city

7. train
8. Ford

9. hill
10. book

11. Oliver Twist
12. Mt. Franklin

13. St. Patrick
14. forest

15. fossil
16. place

17. Vermont
18. Nixon

19. president
20. Texas

GRAMMAR CHECK

Making Nouns Possessive

The *possessive* form of a noun shows ownership. By making a noun possessive, we show that the noun owns or controls something else. To make a *singular* noun—a noun expressing only *one* person, place, or thing—possessive, we add *'s* to the end of the word. This form is called the *possessive* singular form. Study the following nouns. Each has been made possessive by adding *'s* to the singular form of the noun:

the work of the *girl*	the *girl's* work
the song of the *bird*	the *bird's* song
the bottle of the *baby*	the *baby's* bottle

To make the *plural* form of the noun—the form which indicates more than one person, place or thing—*possessive,* we first look to see whether the noun ends in the letter *s*. If the plural form of the word ends in *s*, we simply add an apostrophe after the *s*. If the plural does not end in *s*, we add the *'s*. Study the following examples:

the uniforms of the *girls*	the *girls'* uniforms
the songs of the *birds*	the *birds'* songs
the story of the *children*	the *children's* story
the work of the *women*	the *women's* work

Remember that the *possessive* pronouns—*his, hers, yours*, *mine, theirs,* and *its*—are already possessive. Never add an apostrophe to these words.

Self-Check Test

Fill in the blanks by changing the noun in parentheses into a possessive noun.
Follow the example:

***Example*:**   We went out on _____ boat. *(Stuart)*

                We went out on *Stuart's* boat.

1. (Jack)   Last week, we had a party at _____house.

2. (children)   During the _____naptime, I went for a walk.

3. (boys)   I went to see the _____football game on
   Saturday.

4. (teachers)   The _____conference began at seven and
   lasted all day.

5. (professor)   Few people understood the importance of the
   _____ comment.

6. (Dick/Sue)   _____dog is bigger than mine, but mine is bigger
   than _____.

7. (babies)   The room was filled with _____bottles and the
   smell of milk.

8. (women)   After the fire, the _____store closed.

9. (trees)   The breeze whistled through the _____leaves.

10. (cat)   The ticks were caught in the_____fur.

LESSON TWO: VERBS

By the time you have completed this lesson, you should be able to do the following:

- Identify verbs, and explain the work they do in the sentence.
- Distinguish between action verbs and verbs of being.
- Determine whether an action verb is transitive or intransitive.

Verbs are words which express action or the existence of something in time (being). Whereas *nouns* tell us who or what is being discussed in the sentence, *verbs* tell us what is happening to the nouns. Verbs can be *singular* or *plural*. A verb must agree with its noun in *number—singular nouns* must be used with *singular verbs* and *plural nouns* with *plural verbs*. *Verbs* also express time—they tell us whether the action in the sentence takes place in the present, took place in the past, or will take place in the future. Most verbs form their *past tense* by adding *d* or *ed* to the present form of the verb.

Action verbs tell us what the nouns in the sentence do or what is done to them. Action verbs can express physical action or mental action. We use numerous action verbs every day including such words as: *run, walk, sit, stand, eat, play, laugh, cry, study, and work.*

> *The boys played baseball. (Baseball* is the *direct object* of the verb *played.* It answers the question: *What did the boys play?)*

> *Jane bakes cakes. (Cakes* is the *direct object* of the verb *bakes.* It answers the question: *What does Jane bake?)*

> Naughty *children climb trees.*

> Many *people* in Alaska *enjoy* winter *sports.*

Intransitive verbs are *action verbs* that do not have a *direct object*. These verbs simply tell what someone does; they are not followed by a group of words answering the questions *What?* or *Whom?* Study the following examples:

The boys played. (The sentence does not tell *what* the boys played.)

Jane bakes. (Again, the sentence does not tell us *what* Jane bakes—only that she does.)

Naughty children climb. (We don't know *what* they climb.)

Linking verbs join a *noun* or a *pronoun* with a word or group of words that tell about the noun or pronoun. All of the forms of the verb *to be* can be used as linking verbs. Study the following sentences using forms of *to be* as linking verbs:

Katherine *is* an exceptional student.

The Yankees *were* the winners.

New York *has been* my home.

Notice in the last sentence of the example that the *complete verb* consists of the two words *has been*. Often a verb will consist of two or three words which express *time* as well as *action*. The verb which expresses *action* is called the *main verb*, and the other verbs are called *helping verbs* or *auxiliaries*. Together, the main verb and the auxiliaries form the *verb phrase*. Study the following examples of sentences containing verb phrases:

Mary *has been* living with her aunt.

She *has planned* her trip home all year.

She *will arrive* tomorrow.

PRACTICE

Now that you have completed Lesson Two, go back and review the objectives for this lesson. On a piece of notepaper, in one sentence each, define *action verbs*, *transitive verbs*, *intransitive verbs*, *linking verbs of being*, and *verb phrases*. When you have completed your definitions, look through the lesson to see if you have written correct definitions for each of these. Then complete the self-check test below.

Self-Check Test

Exercise A:

On a sheet of notepaper, identify the following verbs as action or being verbs by writing an A next to each action verb and a B next to each verb of being:

1.	run	2.	laugh
3.	is	4.	was
5.	ate	6.	fought
7.	cry	8.	need
9.	want	10.	be
11.	like	12.	hope
13.	am	14.	are
15.	grow		

Exercise B:

Find the verb in each of the following sentences. Next to the sentence, mark I if the verb is intransitive and T if the verb is transitive. Check your answers with the answer key:

1. Little Carrie loved ice cream with chocolate sauce.

2. Above us, the great eagle soared.

3. Great artists paint beautiful pictures.

4. Very few people carry much cash.

5. The girls played tennis most of the afternoon.

6. Most people enjoy warm, sunny spring days.

7. The two small boys fought.

8. Hunters shot Bambi's mother.

If you missed zero to one of these questions, you are doing extremely well and should proceed on to the next lesson. If you missed between two and three of these, you should review the definitions of transitive and intransitive verbs in this lesson. If you missed more than three, DO NOT GO FORWARD. Reread the lesson carefully and then look at this exercise again.

LESSON THREE: SENTENCE PATTERNS

By the time you have completed this lesson, you should be able to do the following:

- Identify the subject of a sentence.
- Identify the predicate of a sentence.
- Write correct sentences following the *S-V* and *S-V-O* patterns.

Now that you understand nouns and verbs, you can begin creating sentences. A *sentence* is a group of words containing a *subject* and a *predicate* and *expressing a complete thought*. The *complete subject* contains the part of the sentence about which the sentence tells; the *simple subject* is the subject itself. The *complete predicate* is the part of the sentence which tells something about the subject; the *simple predicate* is the verb. A *simple sentence* contains *one subject* and *one predicate.*

The most basic *sentence pattern* is the *subject-verb* pattern. This pattern consists of a *simple subject* and a *simple predicate*. Study the following examples of the *S-V* pattern.

Simple Subject	Simple Predicate
Birds	fly.
Fish	swim.
Children	play.
Babies	laugh.

The sentences in the examples above each contain one noun and one verb. Although they are very short, they each express a complete thought; thus, they are complete sentences. Notice that the verbs in the sentence pattern are intransitive verbs. They do not lead to another word.

13

Another common pattern is the *Subject-Verb-Object* pattern. This pattern contains a *simple subject*, a *verb* and a *direct object*. A *direct object* is a word or group of words in the sentence which tells what the subject did. In the *S-V-O* pattern, the verbs are *transitive*. They lead the subject to a direct object.

Subject	Verb	Direct Object
Children	play	baseball.
Animals	love	shelter.
Cats	hate	water.

The sentences in the *Subject-Verb-Object* pattern give us more information than the sentences in the *S-V* pattern. The first tells us *what the children play*, the second explains *what the animals love*, and the third tells us *what the cats hate*.

The sentences in the two patterns we have discussed can be made longer and more interesting without changing the basic pattern. *Modifiers* can be added to describe the other words in the sentence. In the following sentences, the italicized words indicate the basic pattern of the sentence:

The mischievous, rowdy *children played* for hours on the swing set. *(S-V)*

Delicate, white blossomed *trees grow* straight and tall in the spring. *(S-V)*

Long-haired Persian *cats hate* icy, cold, running *water. (S-V-O)*

Farm *animals love shelter* in the barn on cold rainy days. *(S-V-O)*

PRACTICE

You have now completed Lesson Three. Go back and review the objectives for this lesson. On a sheet of notepaper define the following terms: *subject, predicate, simple subject, simple predicate, direct object, and simple sentence.* When you have completed your definitions, check them against the definitions provided in this lesson. Then complete the following self-check test:

Self-Check Test

Exercise A:

Column I below contains words which may be used as subjects. Column II contains verbs and Column III contains direct objects. On your notepaper, combine words from the three columns to form as many sentences as possible. Be sure to use words from all three columns in each sentence. You may use words from each column more than once. When you have finished, your sentences will follow the *S-V-O* pattern. There is no answer key for this exercise:

I	II	III
Cows	plays	fishing.
Edward	give	tennis.
Children	drink	cars.
Catherine	drive	milk.
Girls	buy	sodas.
Boys	go	shellfish.
Shoppers	eat	clothes.

Exercise B:

On a sheet of notepaper, write ten sentences following the basic *S-V* pattern and ten sentences following the *S-V-O* pattern. Try not to add other words; follow just the basic pattern until you have mastered it. When you have finished, your sentences will resemble the sentences in this lesson. Save this paper; you will need it for Lesson Four.

Exercise C:

Determine whether the basic patterns in the sentences below are *S-V* or *S-V-O* by writing the correct pattern after the sentence. Check your answers with the answer key:

1. Many wealthy people teach their children to ride horses.
2. The two little dogs ran playfully around the yard.
3. Mother scolded the children for spilling milk on the kitchen floor.
4. The students studied hard throughout the school year.
5. Elizabeth wanted a beautiful Persian cat for her birthday.
6. The sweet old lady carried an enormous purse under her arm.
7. For several hours, the two old friends talked.

PUNCTUATION CHECK

Basic Sentence Punctuation

The four basic types of sentences are *declarative*, *imperative*, *interrogative*, and *exclamatory*. Each of these four sentence types must end with the appropriate punctuation. (Remember that every sentence type begins with a capital letter.) Study the following rules for the appropriate end punctuation for each type of sentence:

Imperative

An *imperative s*entence gives a command. This type of sentence ends with a period.

***Example*:**

> Go to the supermarket.
>
> Mark, take out the trash.
>
> Do not let me forget to call your father before he leaves the office.

Interrogative

An interrogative sentence asks a question. This type of sentence ends with a question mark.

Example:

Do you like to go to the movies?

Where were you this morning?

Is Sally staying with her grandparents?

Exclamatory

An exclamatory sentence is said with surprise or feeling. Such a sentence ends with an exclamation point.

Example:

Help! The house is on fire!

Stop! The thief is escaping!

I didn't know they had married each other!

Declarative

A declarative sentence makes a statement. The sentence type is punctuated with a period.

Example:

The two men walked in silence for many miles.

Margaret and Harry dated in college.

All is well that ends well.

PRACTICE

Exercise A:

Correctly identify each of the following sentences as declarative, interrogative, imperative, or exclamatory by writing *D* after the sentences which are declarative, *IN* after the sentences which are interrogative, *IM* after those which are imperative, and *E* after those which are exclamatory. Then punctuate the sentences correctly:

1. Mrs. Murdstone was a pleasant woman with a nice smile
2. Do you like cookies and milk for breakfast
3. Go to the bank and get some money so that we can go shopping
4. People who live in glass houses should not throw stones
5. Help There are five hundred people trapped in a burning theatre
6. Is Christmas your favorite day of the year
7. I love the holidays better than any other time
8. Come to the telephone as quickly as possible
9. Open the window
10. Small children make a great deal of noise

Exercise B:

Now write three original examples of each of the four sentence types (a total of twelve sentences). Identify each sentence as declarative, imperative, exclamatory or interrogative. Be sure to begin each sentence with a capital letter and to end with the appropriate end punctuation.

PUNCTUATION CHECK

Using Capital Letters

Capitalize *proper* nouns. A proper noun is the name of a *specific person, place, or thing*. The following two lists demonstrate the difference between common nouns which name *general persons, places or things*, and proper nouns. Notice that each item of the second list is capitalized:

Common:

book	river
teacher	dog
bridge	

Proper:

Oliver Twist	Mississippi River
Robert Smith	Lassie
Brooklyn Bridge	

Capitalize the first word of each sentence. Always capitalize the pronoun *I* regardless of its position in the sentence:

The big dog was barking ferociously.

It seemed that *I* would never finish, no matter how hard *I* worked.

Capitalize the first word of a quotation:

Marsha exclaimed, "No one will ever believe this!"

My grandfather used to tell his children, "Never go near the water until you learn how to swim."

When the *"he said"* part of a quotation comes in the middle, do not begin the second part of the quotation with a capital:

"That horse," *she said*, "is the most beautiful animal in the world."

Capitalize all major words in titles including nouns, verbs, adjectives, and adverbs. Capitalize the first and last word in the titles of books, newspapers, articles, songs, movies, and television shows. Capitalize all other words in the title except the articles (*a, an* and *the)* and short prepositions and coordinating connectives unless they are the first or last word:

> *The Fourth Kingdom* is a wonderful book.

> John Kennedy wrote *Profiles in Courage* while recovering from an injury.

> *A Tale of Two Cities* tells the story of the French Revolution.

Capitalize the words *Father, Mother, Aunt, Uncle*, etc., while using them in place of the person's name. DO NOT capitalize these words when they follow *my, his, her,* etc.:

> *Father*, may I go to the movies with Fred.

> Terri asked *her uncle* for the money.

> *My mother* is always eager to help me whenever I ask her.

> I asked *Mother* for help.

> I borrowed *Dad's* car for the weekend.

Capitalize titles when they are part of a person's name:

> *King Richard* was a well-loved monarch of England.

> *Queen Elizabeth II* has been on the British throne for many years.

> *Judge Ruford Smith* heard the case.

> *President Washington* was a great leader in the United States.

> *Pope John Paul II* did many historic things.

Do NOT capitalize the title when it is not part of a person's name:

> *The pope* is an important man.

> *The president* of the United States has many responsibilities.

The judge worked all morning.

Capitalize the names of major groups, religious denominations, and ethnic groups:

*The community contains many *Baptists* and *Methodists*.

The *Chinese* are an important ethnic group in California.

Boy Scouts of America is an organization which teaches boys self-reliance.

Capitalize the names of countries:

France, Spain, Greece, United States

Capitalize the names of cities, states, rivers, towns, streets, mountains, and lakes:

Lake Erie is a beautiful site.

My parents went to *Niagara Falls* for their honeymoon.

I grew up in *Hannibal, Missouri.*

Many immigrants from *Mexico* and *El Salvador* come to the United States every year.

Capitalize the words *North, South, East,* and *West* when they refer to sections of the country. Do not capitalize them when they are used to give directions:

The *South* was very different before the Civil War was fought.

I was raised in the *West.*

She lives *south* of the bridge.

Turn *north* when you reach the stoplight; then turn *west* at the river.

Capitalize the days of the week, months of the year, and holidays. Do not capitalize the seasons:

This year, *Christmas Day* is on *Monday, December 25*.

I work on *Tuesdays* and *Thursdays*, and I have classes on *Mondays* and *Wednesdays*.

Capitalize all languages:

French, German, Russian, Italian, Spanish

Do NOT capitalize other school subjects unless they are part of a course title:

I am taking algebra and chemistry this year.

I am taking *Algebra I* and *Advanced Chemistry* this year.

Capitalize the name of God and all pronouns referring to Him. Capitalize the Bible, the books of the Bible, and all sacred figures:

The *Virgin Mary* was the mother of *Jesus Christ*.

The kingdoms of this world are become the kingdoms of our *Lord* and of *His Christ* and *He* shall reign forever and ever.

Capitalize all trade names:

Frosted Flakes, Michelin Tires, Pepsi-Cola

Self-Check Test

The following dialogue has been written without any capital letters. Rewrite this dialogue capitalizing correctly:

"how are you?" called mark to jenny as she passed him on oak street. "i haven't seen you for a while."

"i'm doing fine," replied jenny. "i'm taking french and accounting at boston college, and i have not had time for anything except studying."

"are you taking principles of accounting i or advanced accounting ii?" asked mark.

"advanced accounting ii," replied jenny. "I took accounting i last year. what have you been doing?"

"i took a trip with my parents. we went to paris, france, and london, england. we got to see the thames river and buckingham palace. we even caught a glimpse of queen elizabeth at the english derby. the trip was great."

"it sounds as if you really enjoyed yourselves," said jenny.

"we did. next year we are going to the holy land. we will see all of the places of the bible—the land where jesus christ walked and the places where he died and was resurrected. then we will come back to the u.s. via a flight through berlin, germany."

"when will you be back?" asked jenny.

"not for a while. we have to spend some time in the east while my dad gets some work done. when dad is ready, we will fly west, spend the night in chicago, and then we will come home."

Review these rules for capitalization frequently, and use them whenever you write to ensure proper punctuation of your work.

LESSON FOUR: ADJECTIVES

By the time you have completed this lesson, you should be able to do the following:

- Identify adjectives and the words they modify.
- Understand the role of adjectives in the sentence.
- Use adjectives to make your writing more interesting.

The basic sentence patterns we wrote in Lesson Three were correct, but they were not very interesting. As we saw, however, we can add other words to the sentences to make them more interesting without changing the sentence pattern. One way to do this is to add modifiers called *adjectives*.

Adjectives are words which modify or describe nouns. They appear before the word they modify or after a transitive verb. Adjectives give extra information about nouns and often answer the questions, *"What kind?"* or *"Which one?"* The italicized words in the examples below are adjectives. Which words do they modify?

Which one?

The *tall* man

The *red* barn

The *spoiled* child

The *white* fur

The *dark* cloak

The *green* pajamas

What kind?

Tall men

Red barns

Spoiled children

White fur

Dark cloaks

Green pajamas

Adjectives make our writing much more interesting and entertaining. Look at the following examples of sentences with and without descriptive adjectives to see the difference these modifiers make:

> The man in the coat walked into the store.

> The *tall, pale* man in the *long, gray* overcoat walked into the *corner* drugstore.

The first sentence gives us no information about the man, his coat, or the store. The second sentence tells us how the man looked, what kind of coat he wore, and what type of store he entered. Which sentence did you enjoy reading more?

> The waves crashed against the rocks on the beach.

> The *enormous, white-tipped* waves crashed against the *craggy* rocks on the *sandy, white* beach.

Again, the second sentence provides a great deal more description that the first. The words *enormous* and *white-tipped* modify the word *waves*. *Craggy* tells us about the *rocks* while *sandy* and *white* describe the *beach*.

Comparative adjectives are used to make comparisons between people and things. They show us what something is like in relationship to something else. Adjectives are generally made comparative in one of three ways:

- The suffix *er* is added to the end of the adjective.
- The word *more* is added before the adjective.

A few adjectives are irregular and do not form their comparative forms in either way.

Look at the following examples of sentences using comparative adjectives:

Jill is *smart*, but Sarah is *smarter*.

Bill is *smarter* than Sarah or Jill.

The *superlative* form of adjectives is used to indicate that something stands out above anything else. Rather than comparing two items, we are saying that a condition is true to a greater degree for the word being modified than for any other person or thing we are discussing. *Superlative adjectives* are generally formed in one of two ways:

- The suffix *est* is added to the end of the adjective.
- The word *most* is added before the adjective.

A few adjectives are irregular and do not form their superlative in either way. (The irregular forms of comparative and superlative adjectives will be covered in detail in a later lesson).

Study the following examples of the use of comparative and superlative adjectives.

Adjective	Superlative Form	Comparative Form
Tall	Taller	Tallest
Pretty	Prettier	Prettiest
Peaceful	More (or less) peaceful	Most (or least) peaceful
Beautiful	More (or less) beautiful	Most (or least) beautiful

John is *tall*, but Mark is *taller*. *(Comparative form)*

Henry is the *tallest* person in the class. *(Superlative form)*

Orchids are *beautiful*, but lilacs are *more beautiful*. *(Comparative form)*

Roses are the *most beautiful* flowers. *(Superlative form)*

Janet is *pretty*, but Martha is *prettier*. *(Comparative form)*

Maria is the *prettiest* girl in school. *(Superlative form)*

Arizona is *peaceful*, but Vermont is *more peaceful*. *(Comparative form)*

Canada is the *most peaceful* place I have ever visited. *(Superlative form)*

PRACTICE

Review the objectives presented at the beginning of the lesson. On a sheet of notepaper, define the following terms: *modifiers, adjectives, comparative adjectives*, and *superlative adjectives*. As always, check your definitions with those provided in this lesson. Then complete the following self-check test.

Self-Check Test

Exercise A:

Column I below lists nouns, and Columns II and III list adjectives which could be used to modify them. For each noun, choose the two adjectives which could be used to modify it. Make as many combinations as possible:

I	II	III
truck	paperback	wood
book	glass	red
table	fire	note
vegetable	white	leafy
tree	ruffled	green
dress	fat	old
man	soft	furry
puppy	intelligent	beautiful

Exercise B:

On your sheet of notepaper, rewrite the ten basic sentences with the *S-V* pattern and the ten sentences with the *S-V-O* pattern from Lesson Three adding adjectives to make the sentences more interesting. Remember that the noun markers *a, an,* and *the* are also adjectives.

LESSON FIVE: ADVERBS

By the time you have completed this lesson, you should be able to do the following:

- Identify adverbs and the words they modify.
- Understand the role of adverbs in the sentence.
- Use adverbs to make your writing more interesting.

Like adjectives, *adverbs* are words which *modify*, or *describe*, other words. Usually adverbs modify verbs, but they can also be used to modify adjectives or other adverbs. Adverbs answer the questions, *When?, Where?,* and How? Many but not all, adverbs are formed by adding *ly* to the end of an adjective. Examples of such adverbs include the words *quickly, steadily, quietly, willingly, stylishly, patiently.* In the examples below, all the adverbs modify verbs:

How?

The girl waited *patiently* for her parents to arrive.

The doctor worked *steadily* to keep the patient alive.

All of the food was prepared *well* by the cook.

When?

The ambulance came *immediately* when called.

The banker arrived *late* for his appointment.

The children finished *shortly* before dark.

Where?

The ship's captain called *below.*

Jimmy's mother waited for him *outside.*

When adverbs modify adjectives or other adverbs, they answer the questions *How well?, How much?,* or *To what extent?* Unlike adjectives, adverbs generally do not have a fixed position in the sentence. They can appear before or after the words they modify without changing the meaning of the sentence. In the examples below, the italicized words are adjectives and the words which appear in bold are adverbs which modify them. What questions do the adverbs answer?

The weather for the trip was **extremely** *good*.

The doctor who attended her was **very** *competent*.

By the end of the practice, the food was **totally** *gone*.

PRACTICE

Review the objectives presented at the beginning of this lesson. On your notepaper, define adverbs and list the words they modify. Then complete the following self-check test.

Self-Check Test

Exercise A:

Use each word as an adverb in the sentence that follows it. Most of the words can be converted to adverbs simply by adding *ly*. Other words are ready to use as adverbs. You may have to change the spellings of some words in order to make the new endings fit:

(precise)   1. He arrived at the party _____ on time.

(patient)   2. Her father listened_____to her story of having been kidnapped by space aliens.

(faithful)   3. The man fulfilled all of his obligations_____.

(eager)   4. We waited_____to hear the news from home.

(calm)   5. The child waited_____ for his mother to get him out of the bathtub.

(quiet)   6. Martha _____slipped into the house after midnight.

(furious)   7. As he looked, he saw the hitchhiker waving _____.

(excited)   8. The hostages rushed_____to meet their rescuers.

(well)   9. The food was cooked _____in the four star restaurant.

(smart)   10. She was dressed _____in her crisp new suit.

Exercise B:

Underline the adverb in each sentence below:

1. Harold's parents waited inside.
2. The car sank deeper into the canal.
3. Carmen is now working to earn her bachelor's degree.
4. The man later called his wife to say that he would not be home for dinner.
5. People soon learn that complaining does little good.
6. The minister stood quietly while the bride and groom took their places.
7. A doctor was badly needed in the small Western town.
8. The dog jumped forward into the street.
9. Sometimes, we ate spaghetti for breakfast and pizza for lunch.
10. I recently took up jogging.

GRAMMAR CHECK

Comparatives and Superlatives

Use the comparative form when comparing *two* things or *two* people. When the adjective or adverb contains two syllables or fewer, the comparative is generally formed by adding *er* to the end of the word. Study the following examples:

tall	*taller*
old	*older*
fat	*fatter*
large	*larger*

(When the word already ends in *e,* simply add *r):*

Sally is *older* than Bill.
This rock is *larger* than that one.

When the adjective or adverb contains more than two syllables, the word *more* or *less* is generally used before the adjective or adverb when making a comparison:

Conscientious   Alex is *more conscientious* than John.

Enthusiastic   My brothers are *more enthusiastic* about football than my father.

Make words superlative when you are comparing *more than two* things. For words which contain two syllables or fewer, add the suffix *est* to the word. If the word ends in *y*, change the *y* to *i* and add *est:*

Lovely   She is the *loveliest* girl in school.

Silly   He gave the *silliest* answer.

When the word contains more than two syllables, add the word *most* or *least* in front of the adjective or adverb to change its form to superlative:

Interesting   That was the *most interesting* play I have ever seen.

Beautiful   The *most beautiful* painting in the gallery is in the front hall.

The words *good* and *bad* do not follow the above rules for changing to comparative and superlative forms. The comparative and superlative forms of these words are listed below:

Adjective	Comparative	Superlative
good	better	best
bad	worse	worst

PRACTICE

Make the word in parentheses comparative or superlative as necessary to complete each sentence:

1. (tasty)   This is the _____ meal I have ever eaten.
2. (muggy)   It is _____ this evening than it was this morning.
3. (good)   He is the _____ of the two cooks.
4. (bad)   He is the _____ shot I have ever seen.
5. (enormous)   This tree is _____ than the one down the road.
6. (hot)   It is _____ in this house than it is outside.
7. (silly)   Ben is _____ than Mark.
8. (smart)   Jerry is the _____ person in the class.
9. (brave)   Chris is _____ than Steve.
10. (good)   I had a _____ time, but it was not the _____ time I have had.
11. (bad)   He is the _____ horseman in the country club.
12. (good)   I am a _____ swimmer than you.
13. (good)   I thought my niece was the _____ child in the world until my nephew was born.

GRAMMAR CHECK

Recognizing Prepositions

A *preposition* is a word that shows the relationship of a noun or a pronoun to another word in the sentence. A *prepositional phrase* is a group of words that begins with a preposition and generally ends with a noun or pronoun. The noun or pronoun that ends the prepositional phrase is called *the object of the preposition*. **Figure A** lists some common prepositions:

among	aboard	after	around
about	again	below	before
behind	as	above	along
at	across	amid	out
beside	for	under	outside
from	in	underneath	between
unto	over	past	of
despite	concerning	of	respecting
during	with	opposite	through
toward	within	to	near
throughout	off	until	far
since			

Figure A

The word *preposition* means "placed before," and it generally comes before a noun or pronoun to connect that word—its object—to the rest of the sentence. Generally, prepositions are used to express *space*, *time* and *other relationships between words*.

Study the following sentences. The preposition appears in boldface, and the remainder of the prepositional phrase is italicized:

> The little brook ran **through** the valley and **across** *the farm*.

> The frightened mouse hid **under** *the table* **near** *the box*.

> We paid $25.00 **for** *the flowers* **from** *the florist*.

> Jim stood **in** *the doorway*, calling **to** *the taxi*.

Note*:* Generally it is considered bad form to end a sentence with a preposition. Try to write your sentences so that they do not end in prepositions:

> *Very informal:* He is the person I was talking to.

> *Formal:* He is the person to whom I was talking.

Self-Check Test

Find the prepositional phrase in the following sentences. Underline the preposition once and then circle the entire phrase:

1. Near the door was a chair with a broken arm.
2. Inside the old house stood the pump.
3. The man stood beneath the trees gazing across the starry nighttime sky.
4. Upon her arrival, Mary paid the bill from the doctor.
5. Below the mountains was a tremendous meadow filled with the fragrance of magnolias.
6. Jerry promised to arrive at the station within the hour.
7. Until the man arrived, his wife and children waited by the door.
8. Neither of the children has come to bed.
9. Throughout the school year, teachers stressed the importance of punctuality.
10. Along the road grew clumps of trees with green, waxy leaves.

Use the prepositions listed in **Figure A** of this unit in the next assignment. Remember not to end sentences with any of these words. After the paragraphs are completed, go through and underline each preposition, and circle the entire prepositional phrase.

LESSON SIX: S-V-IO-O PATTERNS

By the time you have completed this lesson, you should be able to do the following:

- Write sentences using the *S-V-IO-O* pattern.
- Vary your writing by using different patterns.

The *S-V-IO-O* pattern is similar to the *S-V-O* pattern that we studied in the last lesson. In the *S-V-IO-O* pattern, we insert a word between the verb and the direct object to show that someone received the object. The word is the *indirect object* of the sentence. The verbs used with this pattern include *give, send, teach, write, buy, lend, offer, ask, and show*.

Study the following examples of sentences using the *S-V-IO-O* pattern:

Subject	Verb	Indirect Object	Object
Mark	gave	me	the reports.
John	handed	him	the roses.
Tyler	offered	him	a job.
Maria	taught	her daughter	the alphabet.
The students	asked	the professor	a question.
My brother	lends	his friend	money.

PRACTICE

Combine the words in the columns below to form as many sentences as possible following the *S-V-IO-O* pattern. Be sure to use words from each column for every sentence you write:

John	gave	me	a letter.
Edward	asked	him	flowers.
Maria	showed	her	a new coat.
My brother	sent	Jan	the message.
Dad	wrote	Mary	candy.
My cousin	bought	Cathy	friendship.
Carla	offered	them	a question.

LESSON SEVEN: S-LV-N PATTERNS

By the time you have completed this lesson, you should be able to do the following:

- Write concise sentences following the *Subject-Linking Verb-Noun* pattern.
- Identify sentences following this pattern.

The verb in the *Subject-Linking Verb-Noun* pattern is a special kind of intransitive verb called a *linking verb*. The *linking verb* provides a link between two different ways of talking about the same subject. The most common linking verbs are the forms of the verb *to be*: *am, is, are, was, were,* etc. *Become* and *remain* are two additional verbs which work well with this pattern. Study the following examples of sentences following the *S-LV-N* pattern:

Subject	Linking Verb	Noun
The books	were	bestsellers.
Tom	became	her friend.
Lisa	was	president.
They	were	lawyers.
The Lord	is	my shepherd.

Notice that the nouns in the pattern all refer to the same person or thing as the subject. The noun provides a label or an additional name for the subject. Study the following examples carefully:

Subject	Link	Same Person
Jeannie	is	my sister.
She	is	a nurse.
Her husband	became	a doctor.
Their daughter	remains	a student.

As with the other patterns, the *S-LV-N* pattern can be expanded with modifiers to make the sentences more interesting. The modifiers have been italicized:

The *old, angry* woman is my *next door* neighbor.

The *famous* attorney is a *very unhappy* person.

Self-Check Test

Exercise A:

Each of the following sentences requires a noun to complete the *S-LV-N* pattern. Choose a single noun to complete each sentence. In some cases, you may have to change the *a* to *an*. Student answers will vary; there is no answer key for this exercise:

1. A run down old car is a _____.
2. Naughty children are _____.
3. Most people live in a _____.
4. Maria went to college to become a_____.
5. Plants which grow where they are not wanted
   are_____.
6. An extremely intelligent person is a _____.
7. An unknown actor may become a _____overnight.
8. People who obtain stories for newspapers are_____.
9. A machine which plays video games is _____.
10. A sweet, obedient child is a_____.

Exercise B:

Now write ten sentences of your own following the *S-LV-N* pattern.

LESSON EIGHT: S-V-O-OC PATTERN

By the time you have completed this lesson, you should be able to do the following:

- Write sentences using the *S-V-O-OC* pattern.
- Incorporate this pattern into your own writing.

Like the *S-V-N* pattern, the *S-V-O-OC* pattern uses a *transitive verb*. This time, however, we add a word which labels the object. This word is called the *object complement*. Verbs that can be used with this pattern include *make, call, elect, appoint, name, consider*. Study the following sentences using the *S-V-O-OC* pattern:

Subject	Verb	Object	Object Complement
Joe	called	Dan	a liar.
The people	elected	Jack Smith	president.
IBM	made	Sarah	a supervisor.
Donna	considers	her brother	a jerk.
The mayor	appointed	you	commissioner.

PRACTICE

Combine the words from each of the four columns to form as many sentences as possible using the *S-V-O-OC* pattern:

Dick	made	Eddie	a scoundrel.
Jane	appointed	him	president.
Rick	elected	Sandra	commissioner.

The people	named	Donald	mayor of the city.
The city	considered	his brother	a thief.
The students	called	Sam Smith	a genius.

LESSON NINE: S-V-O-ADJ PATTERNS

By the time you have completed this lesson, you should be able to do the following:

- Write sentences using the *S-V-O Adj* pattern.
- Incorporate all the patterns into your own writing.

The final pattern is the easiest to use. In this pattern, we have a subject, a transitive verb, an object, and an adjective which modifies, or describes, the object. Study the following sentences using the *S-V-O-Adj* pattern:

Subject	Verb	Object	Adjective
The statement	made	Jim	furious.
Sarah	thought	our ideas	silly.
Boots	made	Jesse	taller.
Sam	considered	Veronica	stupid.
Clint	thought	Mark	ugly.
Veronica	considered	Sam	loyal.

The following sentences also contain the *S-V-O-Adj* pattern, but they have been expanded:

Laughter makes a heavy *heart light*.

Crowds considered heroes great.

The *mayor's* foolish *statement* made the already angry *crowd furious*.

Carla's explosive *temper made Catherine* very *nervous*.

PRACTICE

Combine words from each of the columns below to form as many sentences as possible. Then write ten sentences of your own following this pattern:

The statement	thought	the crowd	happy.
Her temper	appeared	John	silly.
Linda	made	Joe	taller.
Caroline	considered	Sally	finished.
The shoes	left	the room	empty.
The chair	believed	our ideas	ridiculous.

GRAMMAR CHECK

Sentence Fragments and Run-On Sentences

A sentence fragment is a group of words that does not contain a complete subject and a complete verb and which does not make sense by itself. Be very careful not to use sentence fragments. To avoid sentence fragments, be sure that all sentences contain complete subjects and complete verbs and express complete thoughts.

Study the following examples:

Fragment:

Little boys who like to throw stones

The preceding group of words does not express a complete thought. There is nothing in this sentence to tell us what little boys who like to throw stones do. The group of words does not make sense by itself. Therefore, it is a fragment.

Fragment:

> *Eating the cherry pie greedily*

This group of words is not a sentence because it does not contain a subject. There is nothing here to tell us who was eating the cherry pie greedily. Again, the group of words does not express a complete thought.

Often, a sentence fragment can be corrected by adding a subject or a verb (whichever part is missing) or by adding the fragment to another sentence in the paragraph so that it is complete and makes sense.

A run-on sentence is a sentence which expresses more than one complete thought without proper punctuation. If the sentence contains two complete parts without any punctuation, it is a run-on sentence.

Run-On Sentence:

> *We went to school we completed our homework.*

The above run-on sentence could be corrected easily by writing it as two separate sentences or by adding a conjunction.

> *We went to school. We completed our homework.*

> *We went to school, and we completed our homework.*

Self-Check Test

Exercise A:

Some of the numbered groups of words below are fragments. Others are run-on sentences. If the numbered group of words is a sentence, underline the subject once and the verb twice. If the group of words is a fragment, add the necessary subject or verb to make the fragment into a complete sentence. If the group is a run-on sentence, rewrite it as two complete sentences or join the two with a conjunction and a comma:

1. Birds that live in the tropics are very beautiful.
2. People who live in glass houses.
3. Girls who are Girl Scouts sell cookies every year.
4. My cousin could not swim she took lessons at the YMCA.
5. Living alone in the desert.
6. George promised to help his girlfriend with the party he spent all day cleaning the garage.
7. Because we went to the party.
8. I want to become a better writer I practice a little every day.
9. When we are finished with our work, we will be ready to leave.
10. If you cannot get along with your sister.
11. The work is too hard for one person at least two people should be doing this job.
12. To look for his friend.
13. With the best attorney in town.
14. While we were having lunch.
15. The Fourth of July is a special holiday it commemorates the birthday of our country.

Exercise B:

The following paragraph contains sentence fragments. Find the sentence fragments and rewrite the paragraph to correct them:

When I was small, my brother and I spent many happy hours together. Climbing trees. When we were high in the boughs of the tree. We were certain that we could see the whole world. Enjoying the cool breeze through the branches. We could spend an entire afternoon. Then we heard Mother call us and tell us to come down. Because we were not allowed to climb trees.

GRAMMAR CHECK

Regular Subject/Verb Agreement

A singular subject (indicating that only one person or thing is involved) requires a singular verb. A plural subject (indicating that more than one person or thing is involved) requires a plural verb. You must make your verb agree in number with your subject. Remember, most nouns form their plurals by adding *s*. (A few nouns are irregular and have different endings):

One cat	Many cats
One barn	Many barns
One house	Many houses
One towel	Many towels.

The singular form of most present tense verbs requires an *s*. (The *s* ending on verbs is used the opposite way from the ending on nouns.) For most verbs, the form that ends in *s* is the singular form, and the form that does not end in *s* is the plural form. These spelling changes occur only in present tense verbs. Past tense verbs remain the same in singular and plural forms.

Study the following examples. Notice that the singular nouns require singular verbs while the plural nouns require plural verbs:

Plural: The happy *girls play* for hours with their dolls.

Singular: The happy *girl plays* for hours with her doll.

Plural: The *towels need* to be washed.

Singular: The *towel needs* to be washed.

Plural: Most retired *men read* the morning newspaper.

Singular:	My *father reads* the morning newspaper.

Note:

The word *has* is *third person singular. Have* is plural, and it is also the form used with *I.* When we talk about ourselves using *I, we* or *you*, we do not add the *s* ending to verbs. The *s* ending is used only when we talk about someone else—a "third person."

Self-Check Test

Underline the correct form of the verb to complete the sentence. Look first to see whether the subject is singular or plural:

1. Mary, Kathy and Paula (is/are) the leaders of the team.

2. My brothers and sisters (spend/spends) many hours laughing and talking.

3. Few people (has/have) ever seen the Loch Ness.

4. My dog (is/are) the only one in the county.

5. I (likes/like) chocolate cake with chocolate ice cream.

6. They (was/were) the only people on the team.

7. Fred and John (needs/need) a screwdriver.

8. Martha and Marie (search/searches) the house.

9. Kimmy and Betsy (is/are) my two hamsters.

10. *Gone with the Wind* and *Ben Hur* (is/are) my favorite movies.

LESSON TEN: TOPIC SENTENCES

By the time you have completed this lesson, you should be able to do the following:

- Define paragraphs.
- Write effective topic sentences and organize paragraphs around them.

The most basic writing is paragraph writing. A paragraph is a block of information consisting of several sentences which relate to one single idea. With the exception of paragraph writing in personal letters, a paragraph must ALWAYS contain at least two sentences. Never write one-sentence paragraphs.

Paragraphs are easily recognizable if they are correctly set up because a new paragraph always begins on a new line on the page and is usually indented five spaces—one half to one inch—from the left margin of the paper. Every other line of the paragraph should be even, or "flush" with the left margin.

Paragraphs may also be written in what is known as block style. In block style, the first line of the paragraph is not indented. Instead, a space is left between paragraphs, and the beginning sentence of the paragraph is flush with the left margin. Consequently, the entire paragraph looks like a block of text. Block style is most commonly used in newspapers, magazines, and textbooks and is sometimes used effectively in business letters.

Essays and academic assignments should generally be written in the indented paragraph format. Be consistent. Always begin every paragraph on a new line. When writing a document by hand, skip a line between paragraphs so that each paragraph will be completely set off. When using the block style, leave a blank line between each paragraph.

Composing paragraphs is relatively simple. All that is required is a suitable topic. The topic is the specific subject for the paragraph. A topic for a paragraph should be narrow enough that it can be discussed well in a few sentences.

Suppose, for example, that a paragraph will be about dogs. Key questions to ask include: *Will I be able to write a good paragraph about dogs? Just one paragraph? Would the paragraph center around the kinds of dogs, or the size of dogs, or the colors of dogs, or breeds of dogs?* The paragraph might focus on what dogs like to eat. There are many different aspects of dogs which this paragraph might cover. Obviously, the topic *dogs* is too broad for one paragraph because it would be impossible to discuss all of the different characteristics of dogs in just a few sentences. It is better, therefore, to narrow the general topic *dogs* to a more specific topic: *German Shepherds.*

Now the topic has been narrowed considerably. A decision to write about German Shepherds eliminates other breeds of dogs. This topic is still much too broad, however. It must be further focused on one specific German Shepherd. Perhaps the focus of the paragraph should be on one German Shepherd named Max. Now *Max* has become the topic of the paragraph. What specifically about Max is important? Is Max a beautiful dog, a smart dog, a lazy dog, a trustworthy dog, a friendly dog, etc.? Because the paragraph contains only a few sentences, it should concentrate on one aspect of Max's personality, behavior, or characteristics. For instance, the paragraph might explain that Max is a good watchdog. This topic is narrow enough to treat with some detail.

After the topic has been narrowed sufficiently, the next step is to create a topic sentence. The topic sentence is the one sentence in the paragraph which tells the reader what the subject is and how the subject will be addressed. An important question to ask in preparing the topic sentence is "What is the subject of this paragraph?" The topic sentence should answer that question. Usually, the topic sentence is the first sentence in the paragraph, but it can also appear in the middle or even at the end. The position of the topic sentence is determined by the way in which the paragraph is organized.

Topic sentences also help to focus the topic further. Once the topic sentence has been composed, all of the remaining sentences in the paragraph must support that topic. When the topic changes, it is time to begin a new paragraph.

We will now take some topics and focus them into topic sentences. Suppose that we are going to write a paragraph describing the appearance of German Shepherds. The topic sentence for this paragraph might be:

German Shepherds are beautiful dogs.

This topic is focused enough so that an effective paragraph could be written supporting the statement that German Shepherds are beautiful dogs. Each sentence would give specific information about the physical characteristics of German Shepherds which make them beautiful. One sentence might discuss the dogs' coloring, while the remaining sentences might mention their size, the shape of their heads, ears, bodies, physical markings and posture. The paragraph gives as much information as possible about what makes German Shepherds beautiful. After stating the reasons that German Shepherds are beautiful, the paragraph would conclude with a final sentence.

Let us now use this same approach with the topic suggested earlier—one specific German Shepherd named Max. One paragraph does not provide sufficient space to discuss Max's personality, characteristics, appearance and behavior. Instead, choose one aspect of Max on which to focus. Perhaps the paragraph would focus on Max's annoying personality. This topic is now focused enough to make the following topic sentence possible:

My uncle's German Shepherd, Max, is very annoying.

This is the main idea for the paragraph about Max. All of the remaining sentences in this paragraph will give specific examples of ways in which Max is annoying. Annoying aspects of Max's behavior may include incessant barking, digging holes, chasing cars, tearing up garbage, sleeping on the sofa, etc. Each sentence must relate directly to the topic and must give an example of irritating behavior. When the subject of Max's annoying behavior has been exhausted, the paragraph should end.

Topic sentences are essential to keeping writing focused. Without a good topic sentence, paragraphs tend to get sidetracked to stray from the original topic. Topic sentences keep paragraphs simple and straight forward. Be certain, however, that the topic sentence is focused and very specific. If the paragraph seems too general or appears to be getting longer and longer without making a point, it is likely that one of two things is wrong:

- The topic sentence is too vague.
- There is no topic sentence.

In the event that the topic sentence proves to be too vague, go back and rewrite it to make it more specific. Remember that an average paragraph will be between five and seven sentences in length, so choose a topic which can be covered effectively in those few sentences. If there is no topic sentence, create one; then, rewrite the paragraph to support it.

PRACTICE

Exercise A:

Read the following paragraphs. Underline the topic sentences; then, cross out the sentences which do not support the topic sentences. All of the paragraphs in the exercise contain topic sentences, but not all contain extra sentences which do not support the topic. Check your answers with the answer key in the back of the book:

1. I always hated going to the dentist; I suppose that most people do. Needles poked, drills buzzed, and forceps pulled and pushed trying to get enough leverage to get hold of a tooth I knew I would never see again. I did, however, know a dentist, Dr. Roberts, who was a pretty nice fellow. Something gooey or gritty—always bitter and always cold—was constantly going into my mouth. The taste stayed behind for days. By the time my visit had ended, my mouth was swollen and numb, my knees were weak, and my wallet was empty.

2. A camel's hump is not a broken back as some people believe. Rather it is a storehouse of fat which the camel builds up in order to travel long distances in the desert without food. A camel has tremendous endurance and can travel twice the distance of a horse on its long, crooked legs. It has long thick eyelashes which block the blowing sand from its eyes, and it has soft, broad feet which keep it from sinking into the sand. The camel may be an odd creature, but it is perfectly suited for desert life.

3. Have you ever eaten carrot and raisin salad, raisin pudding, or raisin stuffing? Raisins do not grow on vines or trees, as do other fruits; instead

they are created when grapes are dried in the sun. The emerging raisin is a delicious, healthful and wonderfully versatile fruit. Raisins are found in breads, cereals, cookies, sweet rolls, ice cream, salads, and are served with pork and chicken. In fact, they can be used in just about every type of dish a creative mind can imagine.

4. Small children have good imaginations. When left to themselves, they can create an amazing number of stories, games and ideas. In fact, the fewer toys they are given, the more creative they seem to become. When my brother was about five years old, he invented a game called "thin air ball" which was like football without the ball. Although he always enjoyed it, he said it was difficult to know who was winning because he could seldom tell who had the ball!

5. Walking is said to be the best exercise because walkers can work all of the major muscle groups without risking injury. Swimming burns fat and calories in much the same fashion and is relatively injury free, but it can be much more fun than walking. Tennis and golf are other enjoyable sports which provide individuals with the exercise they need. In order to really be healthy, however, people must eat fresh fruits and vegetables and avoid fat and sugar. Exercise does not have to be unpleasant; it can be fun, safe, and extremely healthful.

Exercise B:

Listed below are general topics. Focus each of these topics into an idea which could be discussed well in one paragraph. Student responses with vary:

Example:	*gardening:*	growing roses
	children:	caring for children

1. Texas   2. restaurants   3. horses

4. politicians   5. music   6. hobbies

Exercise C:

Now, for each of the focused topics you have just created, write a topic sentence. Again, student responses will vary:

>   ***Example:***   *Caring for children* is a difficult job.
>
>   *Growing roses* is an enjoyable hobby.

Exercise D:

Take ONE of the topic sentences from Exercise B and write a paragraph supporting it.

UNIT TEST

PART I: Sentence Patterns

Identify the sentence patterns in the following sentences:
1. Boys love sports.
2. Jack gave me the folder.
3. Fred taught the boys jump shots.
4. Jenny considered Mark handsome.
5. Mark handed him the contract.
6. I made Fred the supervisor.
7. The attorney is Mr. Smith.

PART II: Prepositions

Identify the prepositional phrases in the following sentences:
1. Under the chair lay the Persian cat.
2. The little boy covered himself with a cardboard box.
3. Despite the many problems, the business became successful.
4. The children stood in the park amid the pines.
5. The executive assistant went to her desk and wrote a long letter concerning the problems she was experiencing.
6. Tom stood between Sarah and Mark in the class photo.
7. As we celebrate the holidays in the family home, we reflect on God's blessings.
8. Throughout their lifetimes, the people did the things that were right.
9. Toward the end of the summer, we took a trip up the river.
10. Opposite the shore, we saw an enormous black bear with a silver fish in its mouth.

PART III: Capitalization and Punctuation

Capitalize and punctuate the paragraph properly:

> do you want to go to the movies this afternoon asked jeff no
> I'd rather go to the park replied joanne which park queried
> jeff yellowstone of course returned joanne what jeff
> exclaimed yellowstone is over five hundred miles away

PART IV: Adjectives

Underline each adjective in the following sentences. If the adjective appears in the comparative or superlative form, underline it twice:

1. The mailman is tall, but the CPA is taller.
2. The food at the party is the best I have ever eaten.
3. "You are the worst employee I have ever had. We need to have a long talk about your job performance," snapped the irate businessman to his lazy assistant.
4. The dewy red rose lay on the table.
5. Life is good.

PART V: Adverbs

Underline each adverb in the following sentences. Next to the sentence, write the part of speech which the adverb modifies (a verb, adjective, or another adverb):

1. This is extremely difficult to say.
2. We have to have help to complete this very arduous project.
3. It is critically important that this report be filed properly.
4. She combed her hair fashionably.
5. The children eagerly waited for Christmas.

Of all the arts in which the wise excel, Nature's chief masterpiece is writing well.

JOHN SHEFFIELD, DUKE OF BUCKINGHAM,
ESSAY ON POETRY (1682)

UNIT TWO

Descriptive Writing

LESSON ELEVEN: MASTERING DETAIL

Whoever has made a voyage up the Hudson must remember the Catskill mountains. They are a dismembered branch of the great Appalachian family, and are seen away to the west of the river, swelling up to a noble height, and lording it over the surrounding country. Every change of season, every change of weather, indeed, every hour of the day, produces some change in the magical hues and shapes of these mountains, and they are regarded by all the good wives, far and near, as perfect barometers. When the weather is fair and settled, they are clothed in blue and purple, and print their bold outlines on the clear evening sky, but, sometimes, when the rest of the landscape is cloudless, they will gather a hood of gray vapors about their summits, which, in the last rays of the setting sun, will glow and light up like a crown of glory.

At the foot of these fairy mountains, the voyager may have descried the light smoke curling up from a village, whose shingle-roofs gleam among the trees, just where the blue tints of the upland melt away into the fresh green of the nearer landscape. It is a little village of great antiquity, having been founded by some of the Dutch colonists, in the early times of the province, just about the beginning of the government of the good Peter Stuyvesant[1], (may he rest in peace!) and there were some of the houses of the original settlers standing within a few years, built of small yellow bricks brought from Holland, having latticed windows and gable fronts, surmounted with weather-cocks.

In that same village, and in one of these very houses (which, to tell the precise truth, was sadly time-worn and weather-beaten), there lived many years since, while the country was yet a province of Great Britain, a simple good-natured fellow of the name of Rip Van Winkle. He was a descendant of the Van Winkles who figured so gallantly in the chivalrous days of Peter Stuyvesant, and accompanied him to the siege of Fort Christina. He inherited,

---

[1] the last Dutch colonial governor of New Amsterdam

however, but little of the martial character of his ancestors. I have observed that he was a simple good-natured man; he was, moreover, a kind neighbor, and an obedient hen-pecked husband. Indeed, to the latter circumstance might be owing that meekness of spirit which gained him such universal popularity; for those men are most apt to be obsequious[2] and conciliating abroad, who are under the discipline of shrews at home. Their tempers, doubtless, are rendered pliant and malleable in the fiery furnace of domestic tribulation; and a curtain lecture is worth all the sermons in the world for teaching the virtues of patience and long-suffering. A termagant wife may, therefore, in some respects, be considered a tolerable blessing; and if so, Rip Van Winkle was thrice blessed.

Washington Irving, *Rip Van Winkle*

By the time you have completed this lesson, you should be able to do the following:

- Understand the principles of effective descriptive writing.
- Use detail to make your writing more interesting.

The most basic type of paragraph is the descriptive paragraph. Descriptive paragraphs describe the characteristics of people, places, and things. Descriptive writing is used to draw a complete, clear picture for the reader.

A writer is much like an artist. The writer formulates an image in his mind and transmits that image on paper in such a way that the reader is able to see the same image. The writer's job is tricky because, unlike the artist who can use the canvas and his brushes to convey his picture through colors and textures, the writer creates all of his images through the use of words. He can accomplish his task only by using vivid, detailed descriptions of his subject. The more detailed the author's description, the more complete the image will be.

---

[2] submissive

The first step in becoming a good descriptive writer is to become detail-conscious. Suppose that we want to create a story about a woman. The first step is to picture the woman. Although we may already have an idea of what kind of a woman we want to create, we need to take that general idea and create specific details. We might ask the following questions:

Is this woman young or old?

What is her approximate age?

What is her race?

What color are her eyes? What color is her hair?

What shape and size are her facial features—for instance, what about her eyes, nose, lips, jaw line and cheekbones?

What is the length and texture of her hair?

How tall is she? What is her approximate weight? Does she appear frail or strong?

How is she dressed? Are her clothes expensive or cheap?

What is the color and fabric of her clothing?

The answers to these questions reveal other aspects of her physical appearance, personality, and character. For example, if her clothes are expensive, is she wealthy? Perhaps the character has gray hair; this would indicate that she is an older woman. Perhaps she is now a mature, wealthy widow dressed in a simple black dress with a single strand of pearls. Is she attractive or unattractive? Does she seem pleasant and happy or does she appear to be short-tempered and harsh? The more detailed the character is, the easier it will be to effectively describe her.

In the following passage from a short story by Stephen Crane, notice how Crane uses descriptive adjectives to paint pictures of the setting, the characters, and the situation:

> The great Pullman was whirling onward with such dignity of motion that a glance from the window seemed simply to prove that the plains of Texas were pouring eastward. Vast flats of green grass,

dull-hued spaces of mesquite and cactus, little groups of frame houses, woods of light and tender trees, all were sweeping into the east, sweeping over the horizon, a precipice.

A newly married pair had boarded this coach at San Antonio. The man's face was reddened from many days in the wind and sun, and a direct result of his new black clothes was that his brick-coloured hands were constantly performing in a most conscious fashion. From time to time he looked down respectfully at his attire. He sat with a hand on each knee, like a man waiting in a barber's shop. The glances he devoted to other passengers were furtive and shy.

The bride was not pretty, nor was she very young. She wore a dress of blue cashmere, with small reservations of velvet here and there, and with steel buttons abounding. She continually twisted her head to regard her puff sleeves, very stiff, straight and high. They embarrassed her. It was quite apparent that she had cooked, and that she expected to cook, dutifully. The blushes caused by the careless scrutiny of some passengers as she had entered the car were strange to see upon this plain, under-class countenance, which was drawn in placid, almost emotionless lines.

Stephen Crane, *The Bride Comes to Yellow Sky*

PRACTICE

How detail-conscious are you? The following exercises will help you to become more aware of your surroundings so that you can describe detail more effectively. Student responses will vary:

Exercise A:

Look around the room in which you are working. In five minutes make a list of everything you see in your room. When you are finished, count the number of items on your list and write that number at the bottom of your paper. If you are working with another person, compare your list with that of the other person.

Thousands of details in the room were probably overlooked. People have a tendency to generalize when looking at objects rather than really studying them to see the detail. For example, perhaps a clock is on your list. Was the detail on the clock mentioned? Read the following description of a clock and see how it compares to the clock on the list:

> The clock is small—about eight to ten inches around. The back and sides of the clock are black, but the face is clear plastic. On the face of the clock, the numbers 1-12 appear in a circle to represent the hours of the day and the number of five minute blocks in an hour. Among the numbers are short lines—each of which represents one minute. The lines are black and every fifth line is wider than the previous four. The clock has three hands—the hour hand which is a short, wide, black line; the minute hand which is a long, wide, black line, and the second hand which is long, thin and red. The second hand moves continuously while the minute and hour hands move only when the intervals of time they indicate have passed.

Exercise B:

Using as much detail as possible, describe the chair on which you are sitting. Discuss the size and shape of the chair, the materials from which the chair is made, and the color of the chair. Is there fabric on the chair? If so, what is its color, texture, and pattern? In what style is the chair designed? Are there any special features of the chair which make it particularly practical or useful? Think about the way that the chair feels to you when you sit in it. Try to write in such a way that another person can really "see" the chair. When you have finished this paragraph, read it to a friend or family member and have that person comment on the paragraph.

WORD CHECK

Using To, Two and Too

The words *to, two* and *too* are homophones—they are words that sound alike but they have different meanings and are spelled differently. The word *to* can be a *preposition* or an *infinitive*. It is used with the verb in expressions such as *to go, to stay, to work, to fly, to live, to breathe*, etc. It can also be used to begin prepositional phrases such as *to the store, to the market, to the tailor, to the minister, to my house.*

The word *two* is used to indicate number. It stands in the place of the numeral 2:

> We own *two* dogs, *two* cats and *two* turkeys.
>
> Our neighbors had *two* teenagers and *two* preschoolers.

The word *too* indicates *too many, too much,* or *also:*

> Take me with you, *too.*
>
> I wanted to get the hat *too*, but it was *too* expensive.

PRACTICE

Choose the correct word to complete each sentence:

1. (To/two/too) write (to/two/too) papers is (to/two/too) hard.
2. Tell him (to/two/too) come (to/two/too) my office immediately.
3. I have (to/two/too) children.
4. This is (to/two/too) much (to/two/too) handle.
5. (To/two/too) weave a basket, one needs (to/two/too) have patience.
6. Would you like for me (to/two/too) come with you (to/two/too)?
7. I have (to/two/too) complete the (to/two/too) reports before it is (to/two/too) late.

GRAMMAR CHECK

Using Subject Pronouns

You now know that a noun can indicate a *person, place, thing,* or *idea.* Similarly, a *pronoun* is a word which is used in place of a noun to indicate a person, place, thing or idea. Study the following sentences in which a pronoun has been substituted for a noun:

The man walked to the grocery store.

He walked to the grocery store.

In the first sentence, *man* is a noun. The sentence tells us that the man walked to the grocery store. *Man* is the subject of the sentence because the sentence tells us what the man did. In the second sentence, *he* has been used instead of the word *man*. Now *he* is the subject of the sentence, because the sentence now tells us what *he* did.

Subject pronouns are pronouns which can take the place of nouns as the subject of a sentence or a clause. A *subject pronoun* can also be used as a *predicate nominative*. **Figure B** lists the subject pronouns:

Singular	**Plural**
I, You He, She It	We, You, They

Figure B

The pronouns *I* and *we* are called *first person pronouns* because when we use these pronouns we are speaking of ourselves or our group. The pronoun *you* is called a *second person pronoun*. *He, she, it,* and *they* are *third person* pronouns because they refer to a "third party."

As we have already noted, subject pronouns are used as the subjects of sentences. Study the following examples:

Last Thursday, *we* went to the basketball game with Dad.

He bought us cotton candy and popcorn.

I ate until *I* was full.

When *we* got home, Mother fixed tea and cake, and *we* ate while *we* watched television.

She served the tea in her best china cups.

We had such a wonderful time that *I* will remember that afternoon for years.

If your sentence contains more than one subject, be certain to use a subject pronoun.

Study the following sentences:

Jane and I went to the beach.

Dad and he arrived at the office early and worked all day.

Mary, Nancy, and she are buying the gift for Mrs. O'Malley's baby.

Ronald and he will have to contribute some money.

Joan and I are in charge of the meeting.

When in doubt as to whether to use a subject pronoun, simply think of the sentence as if the first subject did not exist. For example, instead of Jane and I went to the beach, imagine that the sentence says, *I went to the beach*. Obviously, *Me went to the beach* would not be correct. Therefore, the correct pronoun is the word *I*.

Subject pronouns can also be used as *predicate nominatives*. A *predicate nominative* is the word at the end of the sentence which refers to the *same person, place or thing* as the subject. For instance, in the sentence, *My attorney is Mr. Jackson,* the word *Mr. Jackson* is the same person as *attorney*. *Mr. Jackson* is the *predicate nominative* in the sentence. We could rewrite the sentence to read: *My attorney is he*. Now *he* indicates the same person as *attorney*. A predicate nominative is always a subject pronoun:

My *executive assistant* is *Jeannie Walsh.*

My *executive assistant* is *she.*

My *sister* is *the woman with blonde hair* who stopped by the house.

My sister is *she.*

The *man* in the dark coat *is the doctor*.

The *man* is *he*.

If in doubt as to whether to use a subject pronoun as a predicate nominative, simply reverse the order of the sentence so that the subject pronoun acts as the subject:

She is my *assistant*.

She is my *sister*.

He is the *doctor*.

Finally, subject pronouns are used when the sentence has been shortened so that the final verb is understood:

Mr. Hughes has been here longer than *I* (have).

Joan is older than *he* (is).

The bank president is more powerful than *he* (is).

My supervisor is more direct than *I* (am).

Jane is a better employee than *she* (is).

Donald does not write as well as *he* (does).

It is, *it was*, *this is,* or *this was* require subject pronouns:

It is I to whom you must speak.

It is she who handles the meeting.

It was he who delivered the package.

It was she who answered the telephone.

Self-Check Test

Rewrite the following sentences substituting a subject pronoun for the italicized words in each sentence:

1. John, Mark and *Henry* went to the telephone company to order service.
2. Vanessa, Nancy and *Joanne* were my best friends in school.
3. My mother's uncle is *John Reilly*.
4. *David* and Harold spent the weekend camping in the mountains.
5. Mr. Connelly has a more aggressive personality than *Jake*.
6. It is *Maria* who took your telephone call.
7. It was *Howard* who reported the incident to the police.
8. *Melissa* and Shirley are leading the campaign.
9. *David* and *Carol* had a picnic.
10. The person answering the telephone is *Walter*.

GRAMMAR CHECK

Using Object Pronouns

Object pronouns are called object pronouns because they are *objects of the action in the sentence*. The object pronouns are listed in **Figure C** below:

Singular	Plural
Me	Us
You	You
Him	Them
Her	
It	

Figure C

Study the following sentences using object pronouns. In each sentence the object pronoun is *an indirect object*, the *object of a preposition* or a *direct object:*

Mr. Walters handed the mail to me.

Frank gave me the assignment.

Joe called him.

We spoke with her.

We will meet with them.

I am calling him right now.

Remember that object pronouns are often used after the verb. In many cases, the object pronoun receives action from the verb.

Self-Check Test

Exercise A:

Rewrite each of the following sentences substituting an object pronoun for the italicized word or words:

1. John made *Fred and Jeff* responsible for cleaning the school.
2. Doris invited *Hilda and Connie* to come to the theatre.
3. Mark brought two dozen beautiful red roses for *Gena*.
4. George handed *Diane* the letters and told *Diane* that he needed them by that afternoon.
5. Cindy sent *Joan, Sarah and Donna* a bill for dry-cleaning.
6. Rita went to dinner with *Harold*.
7. The church held a beautiful retirement party for *Johnny and Marsha*.
8. The school built a new gymnasium for *the boys' basketball team*.
9. People generally like *Sarah* when she is behaving well.
10. Pete and Mary bought ice cream for *Dick and Carla*.

Exercise B:

Choose the correct pronoun in each of the sentences below. Some sentences require subject pronouns; others require object pronouns:

1. It was (I/me) who called you yesterday.
2. She went to dinner with (he/him).
3. It was (she/her) who left the package.
4. Tom, Dick, and (he/him) are planning the party.
5. I am telephoning (he/him).
6. (We/Us) planned the party.
7. The party was for (we/us).
8. Are (we/us) girls invited?
9. This is (he/him) at the door.
10. It is (she/her) you must see.

WORD CHECK

Using Real and Really

The word *real* indicates that an object is *authentic* or *genuine*, as opposed to being artificial. Study the following sentences:

> The lady wore a *real* diamond wedding ring. (A genuine diamond).

> Kraft uses *real* milk in its cheese. (Genuine milk).

The word *really* is an adverb which has a similar meaning to that of the word *very*. *Really* is used to give special emphasis to *adjectives*, *verbs,* or *other adverbs:*

> My father is *really* successful.

> Monster truck shows are *really* exciting.

> Someday I will make my parents *really* proud of me.

Self-Check Test

Choose the correct word to complete the sentence:

1. That is a (real/really) nice tie.
2. When nails get (real/really) old, they rust.
3. The little boy had (real/really) tears running down his cheeks.
4. My sister is a (real/really) big liar.
5. The roses in that vase are (real/really).
6. Although it was only a dream, it felt (real/really).
7. We need a (real/really) good deal to launch our business.
8. This time is (real/really) stressful.
9. Life has been (real/really) good since I started college.
10. Sharon has shown (real/really) improvement in the last few months.

GRAMMAR CHECK

Avoiding Shifts in Person

Do not shift from *first person* to the more general *second person*. This is called a *shift in person* and it must be carefully avoided. Study the following examples:

Incorrect:

> I would like to stay in this area, but you know how hard it can be to get a job here when you don't have much experience.

Correct:

> I would like to stay in this area, but I know that it may be hard to get a job here because I don't have much experience.

Do not shift from *one* or *a person* to *you*:

Incorrect:

If *a person* wants to learn to speak Spanish, *you* must really study.

Correct:

If *a person* wants to learn to speak Spanish, *he* must really study.

Do not use the word *you* in formal writing. Use *one* or *a person* instead.

Incorrect:

If *you* want to do well in life, *you* need to stay in school.

Correct:

A person who wants to do well in life needs to stay in school.

Incorrect:

You should spend two hours studying for every hour spent in a college classroom.

Correct:

One should spend two hours studying for every hour *she* spends in a college classroom.

Self-Check Test

Rewrite the following paragraph correcting the shifts in person. Do not use the word *you* anywhere in the finished paragraph. Check your revised paragraph against the answer key:

If you want to succeed in life, it is important that you remain in school and earn a good education. I know that education really makes a difference because when you go to get a job, employers want to know about your grades. I would like my grades to be as high as possible, because if they are high you will have a good chance of being hired. Studying is important for more than just career advancement though. When you have a good education, you understand the world around you better. In addition, I think learning is interesting, and the more you learn, the more interesting you find your studies.

Review your last paragraph. Did it contain shifts in person? Did you use the word *you* where you should have used *one* or *a person*? Following the guidelines discussed in this lesson, rewrite your paragraph correcting any shifts in person.

GRAMMAR CHECK

Avoiding Shifts in Time

In all writing, maintain sentences and paragraphs in the same time order. Do not shift from *present tense* to *past tense* in the same sentence or paragraph describing only one event. Events being described in the past tense must be kept in the past tense. The same is true of events in present tense. Remember these simple rules:

Do not shift from past to present:

Incorrect:

As I *was talking* to Keith, he suddenly *tells* me that he *is* leaving.

Correct:

As I *was talking* to Keith, he suddenly *told* me that he *was* leaving.

Incorrect:

As I *was writing* my essay, I suddenly *remember* that I forgot to call my dad.

Correct:

As I *was writing* on my essay, I suddenly *remembered* that I forgot to call my dad.

Use the perfect tense (formed by using *have* or *has* with the past tense verb) to show events which *began in the past and are still continuing in the present* or *are having an impact on the present:*

Example:

I *have worked* most of my life.

The doctor *has treated* over one thousand patients.

The *past perfect tense* (formed by using *had* with the past tense verb) is used to show events that *happened in the past before other past events*:

Example:

Janie *had called* before I returned home.

Be sure to use the past perfect tense properly. Do not show that two past events took place at the same time if one actually happened before the other:

Incorrect:

My brother told me that the doctor *called.* (The doctor called first.)

Correct:

My brother told me that the doctor *had called.*

Incorrect:

Jeannie explained that she *heard* from Chris. (She heard from Chris first.)

Correct:

Jeannie explained that she *had heard* from Chris.

Self-Check Test

Rewrite the following paragraph to correct the shifts in time. The entire paragraph should be in past tense when you have finished:

> One day I was out walking when I stop to look at the flowers. Earlier in the day the weather was hot, but by the time I am on this walk a nice breeze is blowing. I looked at my friend Sally, and I say, "Isn't this a nice day?"
>
> Sally replies, "Yes, it's the nicest day I have seen for a long time."
>
> We stand there for a while, and then we turned around and walked back into the house.

Review the last three assigned paragraphs for shifts in time. Following the guidelines presented in this lesson, rewrite them to correct any shifts in time. Be especially aware of keeping the next paper in proper tense.

LESSON TWELVE: DESCRIBING PEOPLE

Nippers, the second on my list, was a whiskered, sallow, and upon the whole, rather piratical-looking young man, of about five and twenty. I always deemed him the victim of two evil powers— ambition and indigestion. The ambition was evinced by a certain impatience of the duties of a mere copyist, an unwarrantable usurpation of strictly professional affairs, such as the original drawing up of legal documents. The indigestion seemed betokened in an occasional nervous testiness and grinning irritability, causing the teeth to audibly grind together over mistakes committed in copying; unnecessary maledictions, hissed, rather than spoken, in the heat of business; and especially by a continual discontent with the height of the table where he worked. Though of a very ingenious, mechanical turn, Nippers never could get his table to suit him. He put chips under it, blocks of various sorts, bits of pasteboard, and at last went so far as to attempt an exquisite adjustment by final pieces of folded blotting-paper. But no invention would answer. If, for the sake of easing his back, he brought the table lid at a sharp angle well up towards his chin, and wrote there like a man using the steep roof of a Dutch house for his desk, then he declared that it stopped the circulation in his arms. If now he lowered the table to his waistbands, and stooped over it in writing, then there was a sore aching in his back. In short, the truth of the matter was, Nippers knew not what he wanted. Or, if he wanted anything, it was to be rid of a scrivener's table altogether. Among the manifestations of his diseased ambition was a fondness he had for receiving visits from certain ambiguous-looking fellows in seedy coats, whom he called his clients...But, with all his failings, and the annoyances he caused me, Nippers, like his compatriot Turkey, was a very useful man to me; wrote a neat, swift hand; and, when he chose, was not deficient in a gentlemanly sort of deportment. Added to this, he always dressed in a gentlemanly sort of way; and so, incidentally, reflected credit upon my chambers.

Herman Melville, *Bartleby the Scrivener*

By the time you have completed this lesson, you should be able to do the following:

- Understand what descriptive writing is and how descriptive paragraphs are organized.
- Create well-organized, concise descriptions of people.

Descriptive writing employs *figurative* language—words that create images or symbols for the reader—and extensive use of adjectives to describe a person, place or thing. The purpose of this type of paragraph writing is to allow the reader to *see, hear*, and *experience* what the writer is seeing, hearing, or experiencing.

Physical description of a person is probably the easiest type of descriptive writing to master. A physical description of a person is a very focused topic; therefore, there is little danger of getting sidetracked. When describing a person, it is best to begin from one point and move consistently. For instance, most people begin by describing the subject's face and head and then describe the body and clothes and finally the shoes. There is, however, no reason that the passage cannot begin with a description of the person's shoes and then his body, and clothes and finally his face. What is most important is that the paragraph not skip randomly from detail to detail but that the subject be described in a clear, orderly fashion that is easy to understand and follow.

Beyond physical description is the description of the person's behavior and mannerisms. In the passage from *Bartleby the Scrivener*, Melville helps the reader to see, through words, Nippers' behavior and mannerisms to portray clearly what type of person he is.

When writing descriptive paragraphs, be detail-conscious. Do not give a broad, vague description of the subject; look instead for adjectives that will tell the reader about the subject. Describe the subject fully so that when the reader has finished, he will have a clear mental image of the person being described.

Study the following descriptive paragraphs. Did the author write these paragraphs in such a way that the audience can "see" the scene he describes?

Sample descriptive paragraph 1:

He had rather regular features; a good mouth; light eyes under somewhat heavy, dark eyebrows; a smooth, square forehead; no growth on his cheeks; a small, brown mustache, and a well-shaped, round chin. His expression was concentrated, meditative, under the inspecting light of the lamp I held up to his face; such as a man thinking hard in solitude might wear. My sleeping suit was just right for his size. A well-knit young fellow of twenty-five at most. He caught his lower lip with the edge of white, even teeth.

Joseph Conrad, *The Secret Sharer*

Sample descriptive paragraph 2:

Col. Grangerford was a gentleman, you see. He was a gentleman all over; and so was his family. He was well born, as the saying is, and that's worth as much in a man as it is in a horse, so the Widow Douglas said, and nobody ever denied that she was of the first aristocracy in our town; and pap he always said it, too, though he warn't no more quality than a mudcat, himself. Col. Grangerford was very tall and very slim, and had a darkish-paly complexion, not a sign of red in it anywheres; he was clean-shaved every morning, all over his thin face, and he had the thinnest kind of lips, and the thinnest kind of nostrils, and a high nose, and heavy eyebrows, and the blackest kind of eyes, sunk so deep back that they seemed like they was looking out of caverns at you, as you may say. His forehead was high, and his hair was black and straight, and hung to his shoulders. His hands was long and thin, and every day of his life he put on a clean shirt and a full suit from head to foot made out of linen so white it hurt your eyes to look at it; and on Sundays he wore a blue tail-coat with brass buttons on it. He carried a mahogany cane with a silver head to it. There warn't no frivolishness about him, not a bit, and he warn't ever loud. He was as kind as he could be—you could feel that, you know, and so you had confidence. Sometimes he smiled, and it was good to see; but when he straightened himself up like a liberty-pole, and the lightning begun to flicker out from under his eyebrows, you wanted to climb a tree first, and find out what the matter was afterwards. He didn't ever have to tell anybody to mind their manners—everybody was always good-mannered where he was. Everybody loved to have him around, too; he was sunshine most always—I mean he made it seem like good weather. When he turned into a cloud-bank it was awful dark for half a minute, and that was enough; there wouldn't nothing go wrong again for a week.

Mark Twain, The Adventures of Huckleberry Finn

Now try writing a descriptive paragraph. Describe a close friend or familiar acquaintance. This is the first step in creating solid descriptive writing.

Self-Check Test

Exercise A:

Think of a famous person who is often on television or in the movies. The person should be an individual whom you have seen frequently. Write a paragraph describing that person. Give information about the person's appearance and characteristics. You may want to include "clues" to the person's identity, but do not state the name of the person anywhere in the paragraph. Then take your paragraph to a friend or family member and see if he can guess the identity of the person being described. Study the sample paragraphs for ideas:

Sample paragraph 1:

> I am a tall, tan male with blond hair and large brown eyes. My favorite hobbies are reading, talking, and watching television. I can run faster than any man or woman. Although I usually do not wear clothes, I did wear a tuxedo to a wedding once. Who am I?[3]

---

[3] Mr. Ed

Sample paragraph 2:

> I am a black female, and I am about eighty-five years of age. I have been in both black and white and color movies. Although we are both very old, my famous boyfriend and I look as young as the day we first appeared on screen. Over the years I have made a fashion statement with my trademark white shoes. Who am I?[4]

Exercise B:

Write a paragraph beginning with the topic sentence: *Everyone turned around when the man walked into the café.* Think carefully about this character. What does he look like? What sort of clothes does he wear? How old is he? What are his mannerisms? Be certain that you supply plenty of detail about the man's appearance. When the paragraph is finished, let a friend or family member read it and make comments.

WORD CHECK

Commonly Misused Words

Their/There/They're

The word *their* is a possessive pronoun indicating ownership. It is used to show that an *item* or *object belongs to a group of people:*

> *Their* house
>
> *Their* car
>
> *Their* attorney
>
> *Their* trip

There is used to indicate location. It is also often used to begin sentences in inverted order. *There* is never the subject of a sentence:

---

[4] Minnie Mouse

Please lay the books over *there* on that table.

There once was a mean, old ogre who lived in a castle on a hill.

They're is a contraction for the words *they are:*

They're going to the movies when *they're* finished here.

Your/You're

Your is a possessive pronoun indicating ownership:

> *Your* dog
>
> *Your* car
>
> *Your* husband
>
> *Your* house

You're is a contraction for the words *you are:*

You're going to be in a lot of trouble when your father gets home.

You're not going to be allowed to eat ice cream unless you finish your spinach.

We're/Were

We're is a contraction for the words *we are:*

We're going to have a party on Saturday night, and we want you to come.

We're the only children in school who made A's on the test.

Were is the past tense plural form of the verb *be:*

They *were* going to the beach, but they changed their minds.

You *were* supposed to be in school this morning.

Its/It's

Its is a possessive pronoun indicating ownership:

> The little dog wagged *its* tail with joy when it saw Mr. Jenkins.

> The tree stretched *its* branches high into the heavens.

It's is a contraction for the words *it is*:

> *It's* a beautiful day today.

> If *it's* cold outside, be sure to wear a jacket.

Contractions are considered very informal. Do not use them in formal writing.

Self-Check Test

Choose the correct word to complete each sentence:

1. (Their/They're/There) wrong, as usual.
2. (Your/You're) a really nice person.
3. (Your/You're) brother is a terrible student.
4. (Were/We're) going to the park.
5. Don't just stand (their/they're/there); take (their/they're/there) coats.
6. The children (were/we're) playing in the street.
7. They (were/we're) a long way from home.
8. (Your/You're) going to have to fix the window before (your/you're) father sees it.
9. (Their/They're/There) keys are (their/they're/there) on the table.
10. (We're/were) the best scouts in the club.
11. Over (their/they're/there) is the kitchen.
12. (It's/Its) really a beautiful sunset.
13. The dog wagged (it's/its) tail when I walked past.
14. (It's/Its) so good to be back that (it's/its) almost as though we never left.

GRAMMAR CHECK

Using Indefinite Pronouns

Indefinite pronouns are special pronouns which can be used as the subjects of sentences. They are called *indefinite pronouns* because *they do not specify who is being discussed* or *how many people* may be involved in the action. They leave us without a clue as to the sex or the number of people in the group. The indefinite pronouns are listed below:

Indefinite Pronouns

all	everybody	none
another	everyone	no one

Singular

any	everything	one	anybody
most	some	each	neither
someone	either	nobody	all

Plural

all	many	any	few
some	both		

Notice that only a few words on the list can be both singular and plural. These words are: *any, most, some* and *all*. Any indefinite pronoun ending in *one* is always singular. Use a *singular verb* form with a *singular pronoun* and a *plural verb* form with a *plural pronoun*.

Study the following examples. The indefinite pronoun has been italicized while the verb appears in bold type:

Everyone **is** finished eating.

Each report **is** perfect.

None of the people **has** called.

Everything **is** beautiful in its own way.

The word in the sentence to which the pronoun refers is called its *antecedent*. The indefinite pronoun must agree with its antecedent in number and in gender (sex). Study the following examples:

Each of the girls *brought her* canteen.

Each of the teachers *has his* own parking space.

Each executive *has her* own assistant.

Neither the prepositional phrase nor any other group of words which may appear between the subject and the verb is considered in deciding whether the verb is plural. Singular indefinite pronouns are always singular, regardless of the extra words which may appear between them and their verbs. Notice also that a plural antecedent may not be used with a singular indefinite pronoun. Thus, it would be incorrect to say, *"Each of the teachers has their own parking space."* Because *each* is singular, a singular pronoun must be used. The old way of handling this problem was to use *his* exclusively. A few years ago, there was an attempt to make writing more gender neutral by using the phrase "his or her" throughout, but this is clumsy and very unnatural. The current thinking is to alternate the use of *his* and *her* when employing indefinite pronouns.

When the indefinite pronoun can be singular or plural, the context of the sentence determines whether the verb is singular or plural:

All of the food *is* gone. (The food is gone.)

All of the people *are* gone. (The people are gone.)

Some of the food *is* poor quality. (The food is poor quality.)

Some of the guests *are* unhappy. (The guests are unhappy.)

Self-Check Test

Read each sentence carefully. Then choose the correct word to complete the sentence:

1. Everyone at the picnic (like/likes) to eat.
2. Each of us carries (his/their) own lunch.
3. One of the tables (was/were) broken.
4. Some of the sandwiches (is/are) soggy.
5. All of the counselors asked (his/their) campers to clean up.
6. Each counselor asked (his/their) campers to clean up.
7. Everybody should take care of (his/their) possessions.
8. Some people left (his/their) car lights on.
9. All of the supervisors ordered (his/their) temporaries to remain on the job.
10. None of the teachers (have/has) reported to work.

GRAMMAR CHECK

Using Reflexive Pronouns

Reflexive pronouns are called *reflexive* because they *reflect action back to the subject*. The reflexive pronouns are listed below:

Singular

myself   yourself   himself   herself   itself

Plural

ourselves   yourselves   themselves

Reflexive pronouns can never be used as either the *subject* or the *object* of a sentence. They are used only to reflect action back to the subject of the sentence. Study the following examples of the correct use of reflexive pronouns:

He hurt *himself.*

We gave *ourselves* a pep talk.

I gave *myself* a chance.

This company can help *itself.*

In each of the sentences in the example, the reflexive pronoun is used to refer back to the subject. In the first sentence, the pronoun refers to *he* which is the subject of the sentence. In the second sentence *ourselves*, refers to *we* and tells us who received the pep talk.

Reflexive pronouns are frequently misused in place of subject and object pronouns. This is always incorrect. Never say, "*John* and *myself* went to the luncheon." In such a sentence, the reflexive pronoun *myself* has been misused in place of the subject pronoun *I*. Likewise, do not say, "They asked *Sharon* and *myself* to attend the luncheon." In this sentence, *myself* is misused in place of the object pronoun *me*.

Self-Check Test

The following sentences contain subject, object and reflexive pronouns. Read each sentence carefully. If the pronouns are used correctly, write a C after the sentence. If the pronouns are not used correctly, rewrite the sentence to correct it:

1. John, Linda, and myself went to the movies, and then we returned home.
2. Because I was not feeling well, I decided to spend the afternoon by myself.
3. Robert asked Mark and himself to attend the party, but them did not want to come.
4. I want the kitchen cleaned properly, so I am going to do it myself.
5. Myself went to work this morning and then to the market to get my groceries.
6. Pete and herself are always going places together.
7. She went to the courthouse herself to insure that the documents would be filed properly.
8. I needed the book, but yourself could have done without it.
9. Karen and myself are going to judge the contest.
10. I will take care of the problem myself, since you seem to be unable to do it.

LESSON THIRTEEN: DESCRIBING PLACES

During the whole of a dull, dark, and soundless day in the autumn of the year, when the clouds hung oppressively low in the heavens, I had been passing alone, on horseback, through a singularly dreary tract of country, and at length found myself, as the shades of evening drew on, within view of the melancholy House of Usher. I know not how it was—but, with the first glimpse of the building, a sense of insufferable gloom pervaded my spirit...I looked upon the scene before me—upon the mere house, and the simple landscape features of the domain—upon the bleak walls—upon vacant eye-like windows—upon a few rank sedges—and upon a few white trunks of decayed trees—with an utter depression of soul...There was an iciness, a sinking, a sickening of the heart—an unredeemed dreariness of thought which no goading of the imagination could torture into aught of the sublime. What was it—I paused to think—what was it that so unnerved me in the contemplation of the House of Usher? It was a mystery all insoluble; nor could I grapple with the shadowy fancies that crowded upon me as I pondered. I was forced to fall back upon the unsatisfactory conclusion that while, beyond doubt, there *are* combinations of very simple natural objects which have the power of thus affecting us, still the analysis of this power lies among considerations beyond our depth. It was possible, I reflected, that a mere different arrangement of the particulars of the scene, of the details of the picture, would be sufficient to modify, or perhaps to annihilate its capacity for sorrowful impression; and acting upon this idea I reined my horse to the precipitous brink of a black and lurid tarn[5] that lay in unruffled luster by the dwelling, and gazed down—but with a shudder even more thrilling than before—upon the remodeled and inverted images of the gray sedge, and the ghastly tree-stems and the vacant and eye-like windows.

Edgar Allan Poe, *The Fall of The House of Usher*

---

[5] a small lake or pool

By the time you have completed this lesson, you should be able to do the following:

- Understand the relationship between seeing detail and describing detail.
- Write interesting and colorful descriptions of places.

Describing places is a little more complicated than describing people. Fortunately, basically the same processes are involved in all descriptive writing. Simply make certain that the focus is maintained. Describing people requires that the focus be on one person. Describing places requires focus on one topic—the place—but there are usually many different subjects within that one place. Take care not to get so interested in describing specific details that the original topic is lost.

The best way to learn to describe places in detail is to first learn to see detail in places. As an exercise, find a place which can be observed without inconveniencing anyone. Choose a place that is not too crowded or hectic. A park, the zoo, a backyard, a restaurant or cafeteria, or the library are excellent places to conduct this exercise. Sit down in one spot, and study everything visible within a one hundred foot radius. Start at the point farthest away and scan the entire area. The first glance will not reveal much, so spend some time really looking at all the surrounding objects.

In a park, the first glance may provide a glimpse of *grass, trees, children, a slide,* and *a bench.* Closer study of these objects, however, will reveal hundreds of little details which were originally overlooked. Whereas the first glance might reveal *grass,* closer examination points out *thick, lush, soft, Kentucky Blue grass, cropped short by a lawn mower with just a hint of yellow from the approaching autumn.* What were first simply *trees* become *tall, spindly, delicately-bent ash trees, with green, waxy leaves and rough, cracked, gray bark.*

REMEMBER: When describing places, focus on several different objects and give them individual attention. Be sure to describe the place in as much detail as possible so that the reader can see it clearly. Study the following examples of descriptive writing. Notice that the author describes each object:

Sample paragraph 1:

The courtyard was a sunny, inviting place with red and white blooming oleander and fragrant rosemary spilling over the weathered stone wall. During the hot summer months, a pair of white-breasted pigeons sat on the wall under the shade of the plants and cooed to each other. Occasionally a small racing gray ball of fur, presumably a squirrel, could be seen darting under the foliage, frolicking in the cool moist soil. In the middle of the courtyard, an old stone fountain gurgled cheerfully as if to welcome and comfort all visitors traveling the paving stone walkway which had been heated to approximate the temperature of an oven by the relentless Southwestern sun.

Sample paragraph 2:

On my right hand there were lines of fishing stakes resembling a mysterious system of half-submerged bamboo fences, incomprehensible in its division of the domain of tropical fishes, and crazy of aspect as if abandoned forever by some nomad tribe of fishermen now gone to the other end of the ocean; for there was no sign of human habitation as far as the eye could reach. To the left a group of barren islets, suggesting ruins of stone walls, towers, and blockhouses, had its foundations set in a blue sea that itself looked solid, so still and stable did it lie below my feet; even the track of light from the westering sun shone smoothly, without that animated glitter which tells of an imperceptible ripple. And when I turned my head to take a parting glance at the tug which had just left us anchored outside the bar, I saw the straight line of the flat shore joined to the stable sea, edge to edge, with a perfect and unmarked closeness, in one leveled floor half brown, half blue under the enormous dome of the sky. Corresponding in their insignificance to the islets of the sea, two small clumps of trees, one on each side of the only fault in the impeccable joint, marked the mouth of the river Meinam we had just left on the first preparatory stage of our homeward journey; and, far back on the inland level, a larger and loftier mass, the grove surrounding the great Paknam pagoda, was the only thing on which the eye could rest from the vain task of exploring the monotonous sweep of the horizon. Here and there gleams as of a few scattered pieces of silver marked the windings of the great river; and on the nearest of them, just within the bar, the tug steaming right into the land became lost to my sight, hull and funnel and masts, as though the impassive earth had swallowed her up without an effort, without a tremor. My eye followed the light cloud of her smoke, now here, now there, above the plain, according to the devious curves of the stream, but always fainter and farther away, till I lost it at last behind the miter-shaped hill of the great pagoda. And then I was left alone with my ship, anchored at the head of the Gulf of Siam.

Joseph Conrad, The Secret Sharer

PRACTICE

Exercise A:

Since it is easiest to describe places most familiar to you, begin by writing a paragraph about the place you know best—your home. Think of the room in your home which you enjoy most. This is probably a place where you spend much of your time. Beginning with the topic sentence, "The best room in my home is_____," (fill in the blank) write a paragraph describing the room. Begin at one end of the room and then work your way to the opposite end going over every detail.

Exercise B:

You are now ready to create a place. We are going to follow the story of the man in the café which you began in the previous lesson by describing the café through the eyes of this stranger. Begin your paragraph with this topic sentence: "As he entered the café, the man's eyes darted suspiciously around the room." You are now looking through the eyes of your character. From his vantage point at the door, describe everything he sees in the room. You may start at either the doorway or the furthest wall, but work steadily toward the opposite end of the room. Do not jump back and forth. Remember that this paragraph is about the café; you are not describing the man.

WORD CHECK

Using A and An

The words *a* and *an* are both *articles* or *noun markers*. We use these words to indicate that a noun will follow. *A* is used when the word which follows begins with a consonant sound. *An* is used when the word which follows it begins with a vowel or a vowel sound:

We went to *a* party given by *a* good friend of mine.

We attended *an* interesting party given by *an* elderly gentleman.

I used to belong to *an* honor society.

We have *an* hour before classes begin.

PRACTICE

Choose the correct word for each sentence:

1. It was a/an) honor to meet (a/an) celebrity.
2. (A/An) exciting moment in my life occurred when I won (a/an) trophy.
3. (A/An) elephant is (a/an) animal.
4. On (a/an) rainy day (a/an) animal seeks shelter.
5. I will meet you in (a/an) hour.
6. Take (a/an) aspirin and called me (a/an) little later.
7. Fighting for your country is (a/an) honorable thing to do.
8. We could go (a/an) lifetime without ever seeing each other again.
9. I will have (a/an) difficult time organizing my files.
10. I plan to have (a/an) good time at the party.

LESSON FOURTEEN: SIMILE, METAPHOR, AND CLICHÉS

By the time you have completed this lesson, you should be able to do the following:

- Define similes, metaphors, and clichés.
- Incorporate them into descriptive paragraphs.

Similes, *metaphors,* and *clichés* are commonly-used elements in descriptive writing. Basically, they are phrases which make descriptions more vivid and give writing a creative twist.

Similes are comparisons of two *people, animals, or things* using the words *like* or *as:*

Example:

> Uncle Ted is *as jolly as* Santa Claus.
>
> Her hand feels *like* cold stone.

In the first example, *Uncle Ted* is being compared to *Santa Claus*. The word *as* is being used to tie these comparisons together. In the second example, *her hand* is being compared to *cold stone*, and the word *like* is used to tie the comparisons together.

Metaphors are also comparisons of two *things, people, places or ideas*. In metaphors, however, the words *like* or *as* are not used to make the comparison.

Example:

> Tom *is* a monkey.
>
> The yellow roses *are* drops of sunshine in the garden.

In the first example we are comparing *Tom* to *a monkey*, but we have eliminated words such as *like* or *as* which would make this an indirect comparison. Again, in the second example we are comparing *yellow roses* with *drops of sunshine* without the use of *like* or *as*.

Metaphors must be chosen carefully so as not to confuse the reader. For example, if a sentence states, "My brother is a football player," the reader will take it literally that the writer's brother is a football player and not merely a big, strong man as the sentence may have intended to imply. An effective comparison of a man to a football player should use the words *like* or *as* in the comparison so that the reader will not misunderstand. The sentence might read, "My brother is as rough as a football player when he is awakened early in the morning." Now the reader understands that the man's behavior is being compared to that of a football player.

A statement such as *Shannon is Carrie's sister* is not a metaphor if Shannon really is Carrie's sister. This is not comparison; it simply states a biological fact.

Clichés are worn out, overused similes and metaphors:

Example:

> *He is as dead as a doornail.*
>
> *He is as fast as lightning.*
>
> *She is as dumb as a post.*
>
> *She is a rock.*
>
> *Happiness is a warm puppy.*
>
> *Life is merry-go-round.*

At one time these sayings were fresh, original, and appropriate. They have been repeated so often, however, that they are no longer original or clever. Clichés should be avoided. Similes and metaphors need to be fresh to give writing a distinctive style.

PRACTICE

Exercise A:

Read the following statements carefully. Decide which are similes and which are metaphors. Write an S after those statements which are similes and an M after those which are metaphors:

1. Martin is as sour as a lemon.
2. The campers were frisky lambs on the camp ground.
3. Mary is a bashful mouse when she is embarrassed.
4. The officer was a tower of fury when the robber escaped.
5. She looked like death warmed over.
6. Her laugh is as piercing as a nail through my eardrums.
7. Mark's face became a beaming light.
8. The thunder cracked like a whip.
9. The children were frightened puppies.
10. The wind was as hot as a dragon's breath.

Exercise B:

Some of the following statements are metaphors, and some are just statements of fact. Write an M next to those statements which actually make a comparison between two things:

1. Jerry is my best friend.
2. Beth is the love of Robert's life.
3. Harry's smile is a breath of fresh air.
4. My little sister is a silly monkey.
5. My boss is a very hard person to like.
6. The baby's hair is silk.
7. The chair is a wonderful piece of craftsmanship.
8. My father is a crab if you wake him too early.
9. The field is an enormous emerald.
10. My husband is a complaining old woman.

Exercise C:

Write five similes and five metaphors of your own. Do not use clichés; be original.

GRAMMAR CHECK

Using Coordinating Connectives

A *clause* is a group of words with its own subject and verb which is part of a larger sentence. A clause with its own subject and verb which expresses a complete thought by itself is called an *independent clause*.

The easiest way to join two independent clauses in one sentence is to use a *coordinating connective* and a comma. The coordinating connectives are listed in **Figure D** below:

and	or	
but	nor	
for	yet	so

Figure D

In the sentences below, the independent clauses are italicized, and the coordinating connective which joins them is in bold type: (**Note**: when you use the coordinating connective *nor*, the subject and verb change places.)

> *Birds fly*, **and** *fish swim.*
>
> *I went to the market*, **and** *then I went to the movies.*
>
> *John gave me the report*, **and** *I gave it to Sally.*
>
> *You may have cake*, **or** *you may have ice cream.*
>
> *Mark got into the car*, **but** *it would not start.*
>
> *Mary wanted to lose weight*, **so** *she went on a diet.*
>
> *I do not plan to go to the party*, **nor** *do I want to.*
>
> *The night was clear*, **yet** *it was extremely cold.*

She hesitated to go into the house, **for** *she believed it to be haunted.*

Self-Check Test

Exercise A:

Combine the following independent clauses into one sentence by using a comma and one of the coordinating connectives:

Example: Mark needed a new car. He borrowed some money from Ted.

                  Mark needed a new car, *so* he borrowed some money from Ted.

1. Alfred worked hard at the market. He had a second job at night.
2. The clouds hung low in the sky. It looked as if it might rain.
3. The old car would not start. It was out of gas.
4. The house seemed very gloomy. Many happy families had lived there.
5. Bill could have gone skiing for his vacation. He could have gone hunting.
6. You may leave if you want to. I need you to stay.
7. Irene spent a great deal of money on clothes. She always complained that she had nothing to wear.
8. We like pizza better than hamburgers. We ordered pizza.
9. I enjoy small dogs. I also like cats.

Exercise B:

In your next writing assignment, join independent clauses into one sentence using coordinating connectives. Be sure to use a comma when you combine independent clauses using a coordinating connective.

GRAMMAR CHECK

Using Subordinating Connectives

An *independent* clause is a group of words containing its own subject and verb which expresses a complete thought. A *dependent* clause is a group of words which contains its own subject and verb but which does not express a complete thought. The dependent clause often begins with a word which makes it dependent on the main clause to complete its meaning. Such words are called *subordinating connectives* because they can be used to link dependent clauses to independent clauses. The subordinating connectives are listed in **Figure E**:

when	before	until	because	though	what
if	whenever	after	as	unless	that
although	while	since	provided	whereas	how
so that	no matter				

Figure E

Study the following sentences in which dependent clauses are linked to independent clauses. In each example, the dependent clause appears at the beginning of the sentence. Notice that when a sentence begins with a dependent clause, the clause is followed by a comma. The dependent clause has been italicized:

> *After the party ends*, the caterers must remove the food.

> *Whenever we have company*, we make an effort to treat our guests well.

> *Because the weather was rainy*, we had to stay indoors.

> *Unless you apologize*, I will not speak to you again.

> *If the weather stays warm*, the roses will continue to bloom.

The dependent clause may also appear at the end of the sentence. When the dependent clause appears at the end of the sentence, a comma is usually not used:

> The caterers must remove the food *after the party ends*.

> We had to stay indoors *because the weather was rainy*.

I will not speak to you again *unless you apologize.*

The roses will continue to bloom *if the weather stays warm.*

Self-Check Test

Exercise A:

Combine the following sentences using the subordinating connectives which appear in brackets after the sentences. Do not forget to use the comma between clauses. Follow the example:

Example: The streets were icy. There were a number of car accidents. [Because]

Because the streets were icy, there were a number of car accidents.

1. The meal ended. We walked outside. [After]
2. Jerry wanted a new car. He went to work. [Because]
3. All the houses on the block looked alike. It was difficult to tell them apart. [Since]
4. The dog is sick. We will have to take special care of her. [While]
5. You go to the party. I will not attend. [Unless]
6. You need a ride to work. Do not hesitate to call me. [If]
7. The coffee is hot. I will have a cup. [Provided that]
8. I try. I never seem to make any headway. [No matter how]
9. You don't deserve it. I will give you a second chance. [Although]
10. You call me. I know that you want to borrow money. [Whenever]

Exercise B:

Now, reverse the exercise. Rewrite the above sentences using the dependent clause at the end of the sentence rather than at the beginning. (**Note**: in some of the sentences you may have to alter the word order slightly so that the sentence will read properly.) You will not need a comma this time.

Exercise C:

In your paragraph writing, write at least two sentences for each paragraph in which you use subordinating connectives to connect two clauses. Be sure to use the proper punctuation. When you have completed your paragraph, circle the subordinating connectives.

GRAMMAR CHECK

Using Adverbial Connectives

A previous Grammar Check discussed how to connect independent clauses using coordinating connectives. A more formal way of joining two independent clauses involves the use of *adverbial connectives*. Some *adverbial connectives* are listed in **Figure F** below:

however	furthermore	consequently
therefore	in fact	indeed
nevertheless	moreover	besides

Figure F

When joining independent clauses with adverbial connectives, use a semicolon before the connective and a comma after it. Study the following examples:

The house on the hill is an expensive one; *indeed*, it is the most expensive in the neighborhood.

Mrs. Rogers did not come to the party; *furthermore*, she did not give a reason.

On Saturday the weather was very rainy; *consequently*, we decided to cancel our trip.

Mr. Hughes is considered a very good attorney; *in fact*, he is the best in the city.

Self-Check Test

Exercise A:

Join the following independent clauses using the adverbial connectives listed in **Figure F.** Be sure to use a semicolon before the connective and a comma after it. Follow the example:

Example: *Jane and Martha were very good friends. They were always seen together.*

Jane and Martha were very good friends; in fact, they were always seen together.

1. The weather was very warm. We decided to take a walk.
2. Marta and John made very good law partners. They had a successful practice.
3. The doctor told me that I needed medication. He wrote out a prescription.
4. Fran wanted to buy a new stereo. She took a part-time job.
5. Yellow on black is the easiest color combination to see. I hate the combination.
6. Christy's mother asked me to bake cookies for her party. She wanted me to serve them.
7. My children are the smartest in the family. They are straight A students.
8. I wanted to arrive at the meeting on time. I left the house early.
9. The house badly needs repainting. I bought a can of paint this weekend.
10. There is no space in the garage for a new car. My husband bought one.

Exercise B:

Practice combining clauses with adverbial connectives in your own writing. Be sure to use a semicolon and a comma whenever you use these connectives. In your next writing assignment, use several such combinations. When you have completed your paragraph, underline the adverbial connectives you used.

LESSON FIFTEEN: WRITING THAT ADDS DIMENSION

It was the very witching time of night that Ichabod, heavy-hearted and crest-fallen, pursued his travel homewards, along the sides of the lofty hills which rise above Tarry Town, and which he had traversed so cheerily in the afternoon. The hour was dismal as himself. Far below him, the Tappan Zee spread its dusky and indistinct waste of waters, with here and there the tall mast of a sloop, riding quietly at anchor under the land. In the dead hush of midnight, he could even hear the barking of the watch dog from the opposite shore of the Hudson; but it was so vague and faint as only to give an idea of his distance from this faithful companion of man. Now and then, too, the long-drawn crowing of a cock, accidentally awakened, would sound far, far off from some farmhouse away among the hills—but it was like a dreaming sound in his ear. No signs of life occurred near him, but occasionally the melancholy chirp of a cricket, or perhaps the guttural twang of a bull-frog, from a neighboring marsh, as if sleeping uncomfortably, and turning suddenly in his bed.

All the stories of ghosts and goblins that he had heard in the afternoon, now came crowding upon his recollection. The night grew darker and darker; the stars seemed to sink deeper in the sky, and driving clouds occasionally hid them from his sight. He had never felt so lonely and dismal. He was, moreover, approaching the very place where many of the scenes of the ghost stories had been laid. In the centre of the road stood an enormous tulip-tree, which towered like a giant above all the other trees of the neighborhood, and formed a kind of landmark. Its limbs were gnarled, and fantastic, large enough to form trunks for ordinary trees, twisting down almost to the earth, and rising again into the air.

It was connected with the tragical story of the unfortunate André, who had been taken prisoner hard by; and was universally known by the name of Major André's tree. The common people regarded it with a mixture of respect and superstition, partly out of sympathy for the fate of its ill-starred namesake, and partly from the tales of strange sights and doleful lamentations told concerning it.

As Ichabod approached this fearful tree, he began to whistle: he thought his whistle was answered—it was but a blast sweeping sharply through the dry branches. As he approached a little nearer, he thought he saw something white, hanging in the midst of the tree—he paused and ceased whistling; but on looking more narrowly, perceived that it was a place where the tree had been scathed by lightning, and the white wood laid bare. Suddenly he heard a groan—his teeth chattered and his knees smote against the saddle: it was but the rubbing of one huge bough upon another, as they were swayed about by the breeze. He passed the tree in safety, but new perils lay before him.

About two hundred yards from the tree a small brook crossed the road, and ran into a marshy and thickly-wooded glen, known by the name of Wiley's swamp. A few rough logs, laid side by side, served for a bridge over this stream. On that side of the road where the brook entered the wood, a group of oaks and chestnuts, matted thick with wild grapevines, threw a cavernous gloom over it. To pass this bridge was the severest trial. It was at this identical spot that the unfortunate André was captured, and under the covert of those chestnuts and vines were the sturdy yeomen concealed who surprised him. This has ever since been considered a haunted stream, and fearful are the feelings of the schoolboy who has to pass it alone after dark.

As he approached the stream his heart began to thump; he summoned up, however, all his resolution, gave his horse half a score of kicks in the ribs, and attempted to dash briskly across the bridge; but instead of starting forward, the perverse old animal made a lateral movement, and ran broadside against the fence. Ichabod, whose fears increased with the delay, jerked the reins on the other side, and kicked lustily with the contrary foot: it was all in vain; his steed started, it is true, but it was only to plunge to the opposite side of the road into a thicket of brambles and alder bushes. The schoolmaster now bestowed both whip and heel upon the starveling ribs of old Gunpowder, who dashed forward, snuffling and snorting, but came to a stand just by the bridge, with a suddenness that had nearly sent his rider sprawling over his head.

Just at this moment a plashy tramp by the side of the bridge caught the sensitive ear of Ichabod. In the dark shadow of the grove, on the margin of the brook, he beheld something huge, misshapen, black and towering. It stirred not, but seemed gathered up in the gloom, like some gigantic monster ready to spring upon the traveler.

Washington Irving, *The Legend of Sleepy Hollow*

By the time you have completed this lesson, you should be able to do the following:

- Effectively describe actions and emotions.
- Create personality for characters.

Because human beings are complex creatures with numerous dimensions, an effective description of a person must go beyond mere physical attributes. It must also include the thoughts, feelings, and actions of the individual. Certain creatures are known to behave in a particular way or to display certain personality or emotional characteristics which are commonly associated with those creatures. For example, foxes are known to be sly, cats are known to be agile, bears are known to be ferocious, and dolphins are generally considered to be friendly. People are also labeled with general personality traits: for instance, many of us tend to believe that the police are protective, lawyers are dishonest, politicians do not tell the truth, mothers are nurturing, and Santa Claus is jolly. These labels are called *stereotypes* because we apply them to groups and assume that they fit every individual in that group. Making such generalizations is natural, but it is important to remember that such stereotypes usually are not accurate. When we are discussing or describing individuals, we must look beyond the stereotype to understand the individual qualities of the person being described.

One of the first steps in creating a fictional character is deciding whether that character is going to be *stereotypical* or whether the personality and characteristics of the individual will shine through. Generally, writing is more professional and true to life if the characters have both strengths and weaknesses and possess good points and bad points. The following questions can provide the basis for the character's personality:

Is this character a hero or a villain, or is he something in between these two extremes?

Is the character basically good-natured or bad-natured?

Is the character really weak, indecisive, and cowardly, or is he strong but quiet?

Does the character have integrity and strong moral fiber, or is he basically immoral or amoral?

Is the character going to be the object of a romantic interest? What personality characteristics will contribute to that romantic interest?

If the character will be a villain, what type of villain will he be? Will he be sly, clever, deceitful, backbiting, and thoroughly evil but at the same time extremely intelligent? Perhaps the character will be basically evil and immoral but at the same time an incompetent idiot who constantly tries to harm others but is too bungling and stupid to ever really succeed.

The answers to these questions will determine whether the character is one who can really capture the interest and attention of the reader. After determining how many dimensions the character will have, create the personality and emotions that will bring that character to life for the reader.

The character's actions demonstrate what type of person he is. For instance, perhaps the character is very shy. What actions are associated with a shy person? Think of a shy person. How does that person walk, talk, and relate to other people? What mannerisms does that person have that let people know that he is shy? The description of the character should incorporate actions to demonstrate shyness.

Now, try the opposite approach. Suppose that the story is about a character who is extremely outgoing. Think of a person who is outgoing and very popular. What does that person do to let others know that he likes people? The outgoing character should exhibit those same traits. Perhaps the character is a man who smiles constantly, is quick to speak to others, and addresses them in an elevated tone of voice. How does this person walk, talk, and conduct himself? What mannerisms does this person have? How might this person behave in crowds with many people around him?

Suppose that in the story, the shy young girl and the very outgoing young man meet. What will happen? What kind of a conversation would they have? Would the two characters like each other? What would happen in real life? Try writing a story in which two people like those described above do meet. Discuss how the actions of each character alert the other character to his or her personality traits.

Study the following passages. The authors demonstrate each action of their characters in detail:

Sample passage 1:

> The youth awakened slowly. He came gradually back to a position from which he could regard himself. For moments he had been scrutinizing his person in a dazed way as if he had never before seen himself. Then he picked up his cap from the ground. He wriggled in his jacket to make a more comfortable fit, and kneeling relaced his shoe. He thoughtfully mopped his reeking features.
>
> So it was all over at last! The supreme trial had been passed. The red, formidable difficulties of war had been vanquished.
>
> He went into an ecstasy of self-satisfaction. He had the most delightful sensations of his life. Standing as if apart from himself, he viewed that last scene. He perceived that the man who had fought thus was magnificent.
>
> He felt that he was a fine fellow. He saw himself even with those ideals which he had considered as far beyond him. He smiled in deep gratification.
>
> Upon his fellows he beamed tenderness and good will. "Gee! ain't it hot, hey?" he said affably to a man who was polishing his streaming face with his coat sleeves.
>
> "You bet!" said the other, grinning sociably. "I never seen sech dumb hotness." He sprawled out luxuriously on the ground. "Gee, yes! An' I hope we don't have no more fightin' till a week from Monday."

There were some handshakings and deep speeches with men whose features were familiar, but with whom the youth now felt the bonds of tied hearts. He helped a cursing comrade to bind up a wound of the shin.

But, of a sudden, cries of amazement broke out along the ranks of the new regiment. "Here they come ag'in! Here they come ag'in!" The man who had sprawled upon the ground started up and said, "Gosh!"

The youth turned quick eyes upon the field. He discerned forms begin to swell in masses out of a distant wood. He again saw the tilted flag speeding forward.

Stephen Crane, *The Red Badge of Courage*

Sample passage 2:

They put forth the efforts of a pair walking bowed against a strong wind. Potter was about to raise a finger to point the first appearance of the new home when, as they circled the corner they came face to face with a man in a maroon-coloured shirt, who was feverishly pushing cartridges into a large revolver. Upon the instant the man dropped his revolver to the ground and, like lightning, whipped another from its holster. The second weapon was aimed at the bridegroom's chest.

There was a silence. Potter's mouth seemed to be merely a grave for his tongue. He exhibited an instinct to at once loosen his arm from the woman's grip, and he dropped the bag to the sand. As for the bride, her face had gone as yellow as old cloth.

Stephen Crane, *The Bride Comes to Yellow Sky*

PRACTICE

In order to create effective emotional and personal traits for characters, it is necessary to first understand how to describe the emotions in such a way that the reader can feel what the characters are feeling. The following exercises are designed to increase awareness of emotions:

Exercise A:

On your paper list at least five emotions. Your list may include such words as *love, happiness, despair, sadness, anger, confusion, frustration, embarrassment,* and *loneliness.* If you are working with another person, compare your list to that of your classmate. Think about what it means to feel these emotions. For instance, when a person says to you that he feels *happy* or *sad* or *angry*, what is that person really experiencing? What *physical sensations* are associated with these *emotional sensations*? When you become nervous, do your palms sweat and do you feel as though there are butterflies in your stomach? When you are angry, do you feel hot and as though all of your muscles have become tense? When you are frightened, do you feel cold? Does the hair stand up on the back of your neck? For each of the five emotions you listed, list at least two physical sensations which can be associated with that emotion.

Exercise B:

Imagine that you have just met a creature from outer space. This creature has no emotions; he feels only physical sensations. He does not understand human emotions, and he has asked you to explain them to him. Remember that since this creature has no emotions, you may not use other emotional words in your description. To describe *anger* you may not say: "When you are *angry* you feel *furious* and *mad*," because you would then have to describe what it means to feel furious and mad. You must, instead, equate the emotions to the physical sensations associated with them.

Exercise C:

Return to the description of the man in the café which you began in the last lesson. You are now ready to give your character a personality. Describe the characteristics which demonstrate what kind of person he is. Use the topic sentence in the model below, but fill in the blank with your own adjective. In the remaining sentences of the paragraph describe his physical actions which indicate that he feels the emotion you have indicated. Follow the model:

Topic Sentence: Any observer could plainly see that the man who had come into the café was (frightened).

***Sample paragraph*:**

> Any observer could plainly see that the man who had come into the café was frightened. Upon entering he glanced furtively around the café as though he were afraid that he might see some enemy from his past. When he had taken his seat, he pulled his cap lower over his eyes so that he would not be recognized. He sat with his back to the wall and ate his food hurriedly. When he had finished his meal, he jumped up from the table and rushed out into the night.

UNIT TEST

PART I: Coordinating Connectives

Combine the following independent clauses into one sentence using a comma and a coordinating connective:

1. Jeffrey has a pair of new tennis shoes. He also has a new jacket.
2. You may do whatever you like. If you help me, I would appreciate it.
3. We can spend the weekend at the lake. We can spend it in the mountains.
4. We have acquired all the things we wanted. We still are not satisfied.
5. The family experienced many hardships. They survived them all.
6. Life is hard. God is good.
7. We may have hot dogs. We may have pizza.

PART II: Shifts in Time and Person

Correct the shifts in time and person in the following paragraph. Some sentences may require quite a bit of revision to correct the shifts:

> I have really learned to appreciate my family because you never know what can happen in life. You can wake up one morning, and someone you love can be gone forever. I experienced this when my mother was in a nearly fatal accident two years ago. I get up one morning, and she tells me good-bye. Before I get home that night she has been rushed to the hospital and is having emergency surgery. As a result of this experience, I learned that you cannot take anything for granted.

PART III: Subject and Object Pronouns

Read the following sentences and determine whether the pronouns are used correctly. If the sentence is correct as written, write a C after it. If the sentence is not correct, rewrite it using the proper pronouns:

110

1. Between you and I, John is very incompetent.
2. Jane, Shirley, and me are going to the movies.
3. Peter brought lunch for Sally and me.
4. Us girls are going to the movies with Harry and he.
5. It is me at the door.
6. The fight involved him and her.
7. People needed to know if he were the suspect or if the suspect were her.
8. Jeff is a better employee than him.
9. The person at the door was him.
10. If John and I were in your position, we would be very upset.

PART IV: Indefinite Pronouns

Read the sentences below. If the pronouns are used correctly, write a C after the sentence. If the pronouns are incorrect, rewrite the sentence properly:

1. Everyone likes Mr. Howard.
2. All of the people needs to be treated with respect.
3. Some of the people is displeased with the decision.
4. Each of the teachers brought their own lunch.
5. All of the men is being held accountable for the actions of one.

PART V: Adverbial Connectives

Combine the following sentences using adverbial connectives. If necessary, refer to the list of adverbial connectives found in this unit:

1. Bob and his employers could not agree on the money they owed him. They went to court.
2. The judge ruled that Bob was right. He ordered the company to pay Bob $50,000.00.
3. The company appealed the judge's decision. Bob did not get any money until the appeal was decided.

4. The appeals' court agreed with the judge's original ruling. They ordered the company to pay Bob immediately.
5. Bob received all of his money. He continued to work for the company.

PART VI: Essay

Write a two-paragraph essay describing a person you know well. In the first paragraph, provide a detailed physical description. In the second paragraph, describe the personality of your subject. When you have finished, give your essay to the person you are describing, and ask him to comment on it.

Blot out, correct, insert, refine,
Enlarge, diminish, interline;
Be mindful, when invention fails,
To scratch your head and bite your nails.

JONATHAN SWIFT, *ON POETRY* (1712)

UNIT THREE

Writing that Tells a Story

LESSON SIXTEEN: BASICS OF NARRATIVE WRITING

Once upon a time—of all the good days in the year, on Christmas Eve—old Scrooge sat busy in his counting-house. It was cold, bleak, biting weather: foggy withal: and he could hear the people in the court outside, go wheezing up and down, beating their hands upon their breasts, and stamping their feet upon the pavement stones to warm them. The city clocks had only just gone three, but it was quite dark already—it had not been light all day—and candles were flaring in the windows of the neighbouring offices, like ruddy smears upon the palpable brown air. The fog came pouring in at every chink and keyhole, and was so dense without, that although the court was of the narrowest, the houses opposite were mere phantoms. To see the dingy cloud come drooping down, obscuring everything, one might have thought that Nature lived hard by, and was brewing on a large scale.

The door of Scrooge's counting-house was open that he might keep his eye upon his clerk, who in a dismal little cell beyond, a sort of tank, was copying letters. Scrooge had a very small fire, but the clerk's fire was so very much smaller that it looked like one coal. But he couldn't replenish it, for Scrooge kept the coal-box in his own room; and so surely as the clerk came in with the shovel, the master predicted that it would be necessary for them to part. Wherefore the clerk put on his white comforter, and tried to warm himself at the candle; in which effort, not being a man of a strong imagination, he failed.

Charles Dickens, *A Christmas Carol*

By the time you have completed this lesson, you should be able to do the following:

- Understand the principles of good narrative writing.
- Use time order to record past events.

To narrate is to tell a story; thus, *narrative writing* is writing that tells a story. Novels and many magazine articles are written in narrative style—thoughts, ideas, and events are compiled and organized in such a way that they tell a story. All narrative writing has a *narrator*, or storyteller, who tells the story from his *point of view*. If the narrator is a character in the story, the story is told from *first-person point of view*. The first-person narrator refers to himself as *I* and other characters as *he*. If the narrator is an outside observer, the story is said to be written in *third-person point of view*. A *limited third-person narrator* tells the readers what *one character* says, thinks, does, and feels. Such a narrator can tell what the other characters do and say but not what they think and feel. An *all-knowing third-person narrator* tells the reader what *every character* says, thinks, does, and feels. First person is used in *autobiographical writing*—stories which people write about their own lives—while third person is used in *biographical writing*, in which the author writes about the life of someone else. (*Second-person*, in which the author writes about *you*, is not practical for narrative writing.)

The writing assignments which have been assigned so far in this course have required narrative writing. Although the writing was also descriptive—providing physical details about people, places, and things—it was written in a story-telling format and, thus, was narrative. Good narrative writing makes use of vivid description to make the story interesting. Study the following examples of narrative writing. What makes these excerpts interesting?

Sample passage 1:

> He listened some more; then he came tiptoeing down and stood right between us; we could a touched him, nearly. Well, likely it was minutes and minutes that there warn't a sound, and we all there so close together. There was a place on my ankle that got to itching; but I dasn't scratch it; and then my ear begun to itch; and next my back, right between my shoulders. Seemed like I'd die if I couldn't scratch. Well, I've noticed that thing plenty times since. If you are with the quality, or at a funeral, or trying to go to sleep when you ain't sleepy—if you are anywheres where it won't do for you to scratch, why you will itch all over in upwards of a thousand places.

Mark Twain, *The Adventures of Huckleberry Finn*

I am a rather elderly man. The nature of my avocations, for the last thirty years, has brought me into more than ordinary contact with what would seem an interesting and somewhat singular set of men, of whom, as yet, nothing, that I know of, has ever been written—I mean, the law-copyists, or scriveners. I have known very many of them, professionally and privately, and if I pleased, could relate divers histories, at which good-natured gentlemen might smile, and sentimental souls might weep. But I waive the biographies of all other scriveners, for a few passages in the life of Bartleby, who was a scrivener, the strangest I ever saw, or heard of. While, of other law-copyists, I might write the complete life, of Bartleby nothing of that sort can be done. I believe that no materials exist for a full and satisfactory biography of this man. It is an irreparable loss to literature. Bartleby was one of those beings of whom nothing is ascertainable, except from the original sources, and, in his case, those are very small. What my own astonished eyes saw of Bartleby, that is all I know of him, except, indeed, one vague report, which will appear in the sequel.

Herman Melville, *Bartleby the Scrivener*

Narrative writing can be based on a true story, or it can be fictional, or it can be a combination of both—taking some true incidents and real-life people and placing them in fictional situations. Remember that the primary purpose of narrative writing is to entertain, so narrative works often encompass a wide range of moods from light and comical, to refreshing and inspiring, to emotional and tear-jerking. The pace and the mood of the story are determined by the author who sets the scene to fit his intentions and purpose. Narrative writing offers a considerable amount of freedom because there are no hard and fast rules governing how a story should be told, what type of story should be told, how long the story should be, or how complicated it should become. These decisions are made by the writer.

One element which must be observed in narrative writing is *time order.* Before beginning writing, decide on the time order for the story, and then move consistently from one event to the next in that order. For example, if the story centers around a fictional character, decide when the action should begin. If the action should begin in the morning, write about the first event that takes place in this character's day, and then move to the next event of importance and so forth.

Some writers use a type of time order called *flashback* or *inverted* order. In this type of time order, the story opens *after the main action has already taken place*. For instance, the story may open as the main character is about to be hanged. The author may discuss the sentencing of the character and describe the scene as he is led out of the courtroom. At this point, however, the reader has no idea why the character is about to be hanged or what has happened to bring him to this situation. The author then tells the story in flashback, starting with the first important event that happened to bring the character to this current predicament.

Be aware that once the starting point for the story has been established, the story must move consistently from that point on. **Do not jump around!** If events are taken out of the order of their occurrence, the reader will not be able to follow the story.

It is easiest for a beginning writer to start with the first event which is important to the story and then work his way toward the last event of importance. If, during the creation of the story, an important detail is omitted, go back and insert it at the correct place. Never add details to the end of the story.

The following paragraph is from *Bartleby the Scrivener*. Study the way that each event leads to another. If the events in this paragraph were taken out of order, the story would not make sense:

Sample passage 1:

> Now, one Sunday morning I happened to go to Trinity Church, to hear a celebrated preacher, and finding myself rather early on the ground I thought I would walk around to my chambers for a while. Luckily I had my key with me; but upon applying it to the lock, I found it resisted by something inserted from the inside. Quite surprised, I called out; when to my consternation a key was turned from within; and thrusting his lean visage at me, and holding the door ajar, the apparition of Bartleby appeared in his shirt sleeves, and otherwise in a strangely tattered deshabille[6], saying quietly that

---

[6] a state of very casual dress

he was sorry, but he was deeply engaged just then, and—preferred not admitting me at present. In a brief word or two, he moreover added, that perhaps I had better walk around the block two or three times, and by that time he would probably have concluded his affairs.

Herman Melville, Bartleby the Scrivener

The sample paragraph below is from a children's story. The time order is very carefully organized so that the story is easy to follow:

Sample passage 2:

The sun was shining through Joy McAloon's bedroom window, but she did not move from her big white bed. There was no reason to get up. It was going to be a boring day.

School had closed for summer vacation a week earlier, and yesterday Joy's best friend had gone to visit her Grandmother for two weeks. The town's swimming pool was closed for repairs and the amusement park was only open on weekends. Even though it was only 7:00 A.M., the air was already hot and sticky.

Joy could hear her little brother, Andy, running in the hallway, and soon he burst through her door and jumped onto her bed. "Get up," Andy demanded. "I'm hungry."

The smell of pancakes and bacon came from the kitchen, and Joy felt hungry too.

"Okay," Joy answered. "Go on down to breakfast, and I'll be there in a minute."

Joy put on a green tank top and a pair of white shorts and brushed her long hair into a pony tail before running downstairs. Daddy had already left for work, and Andy was sitting at the kitchen table taking huge bites of the warm pancakes. He looked up at her and smiled as a big drop of maple syrup ran down his chin.

Mama smiled at Joy and handed her a plate of food. While she ate her breakfast, Joy tried to think of something for her and Andy to do, but it was no use. This was going to be a boring day.

Joyce Swann, The McAloons: A Horse Called
Lightning & A House of Clowns

PRACTICE

The following exercises test your ability to create narrative writing of your own. Follow the assignment, but try to be as creative as possible:

Exercise A:

This is an exercise in first-person narrative writing. Think of the most frightening experience you have ever had. What were the circumstances? What did you do? How did you feel? Write your experience into a short story using vivid description. Describe your physical surroundings, the people, and how you felt during this experience. Use good time order.

Exercise B:

This is an exercise in third-person narrative writing. Write two paragraphs beginning the first one with the topic sentence. "On the other side of the hill, he (or she) heard a strange noise." Write about how the character responded to the noise, what he saw, and how he reacted to it. Be very descriptive, and use your imagination to make this paragraph as interesting as possible. This story may be as far-fetched as you like. Be sure to use time order in moving from one event to the next.

WORD CHECK

Commonly Misused Words

Beside/Besides

Beside is a word meaning *next to* or *near:*

> Come sit *beside* me on the couch so that we can talk.
>
> Jan is standing *beside* Mark and Chris.

Besides is a word meaning *other than, moreover,* or *in addition to*:

No one *besides* me came to the party.

Besides Jan there were ten other people who wrote letters of protest.

In/Into

The word *in* means to be physically located in a particular place or to be caught up in a particular situation:

The microwave and the oven are *in* the kitchen.

All of the bookkeeping is *in* a state of confusion.

Use the word *into* when you are talking about entering a room or a place:

If you will come *into* the living room, I will show you my new aquarium.

John walked right *into* the glass door.

Hear/Here

Here is used to indicate the physical location of an object nearby or the relative closeness of an event in time. It is also used to begin sentences in inverted order. *Here* is never the subject of a sentence:

The time is *here* at last for our petitions to be granted.

Set the vase *here* on the desk.

Here is a man with a strong will and a determined spirit.

Hear is a verb meaning to listen to an audible sound. Remember: you *hear* with your *ear*:

Can you *hear* the little robins singing in the trees?

I *hear* every word you say.

Effect/Affect

Effect is a noun meaning the result of an event:

The *effects* of the hurricane were disastrous.

The presence of British soldiers in their town had a terrible *effect* on the Bostonians.

Affect is a verb meaning *to influence* or *to create:*

If coffee *affects* you so adversely, you should stop drinking it.

She had *affected* a foreign accent which made her sound very phony.

Self-Check Test

Choose the correct word to complete each sentence:

1. No one (beside/besides) me went to Jane's house.
2. That is (beside/besides) the point.
3. Go (into/in) the den and have a seat.
4. The fish swam (in/into) the aquarium.
5. The gang with which my son associates has had a bad (affect/effect) on him.
6. The doctor believed that the medicine had dangerous (affects/effects).
7. Reading the newspaper can (affect/effect) our view of the world.
8. (Here/Hear) is where George Washington slept.
9. If you can (hear/here) me, you had better answer immediately.
10. I moved (hear/here) from Los Angeles two years ago.

GRAMMAR CHECK

Using Relative Pronouns

Relative pronouns are used to join special clauses called *relative clauses*. These clauses modify nouns. The relative pronouns are listed in **Figure G**:

who	whom	whose	which	that

Figure G

Use *who* and *whom* when you are referring to people. Use *which* to refer to ideas and things. *Whose* shows ownership by people and things. *That* also refers to things.

Study the uses of *who, which,* and *that* in the following examples. *Who* and *whom* will be covered in the next Word Check. The relative pronouns appear in bold. The relative clauses they introduce are italicized:

> I talked to the reporter **who** *wrote the story*.

> My dog **that** *ran away* was the sweetest dog in the world.

> Mary Jones, **whose** *father was the mayor of the city*, returned my call.

> People **who** *live in glass houses* should not throw stones.

In each of the sentences in the example, the relative clause gives information about the word it modifies. In the first sentence, the phrase *who wrote the story* identifies the reporter. In the second sentence, the phrase *that ran away* identifies the dog. The clauses in the remaining two sentences identify *Mary Jones* and *People* respectively. The relative clause gives extra information which helps the reader to identify the person or thing being discussed.

Self-Check Test

Fill in the blanks with *who, which, that,* or *whose*. Follow the example:

Example: My best friend is the girl_____lives down the street.

Answer: *who*

1. I used to own a dog_____was named Victoria.
2. Later, I had a sister _____was named Victoria.
3. People_____dogs have human names can get very confused.
4. I once met a man_____had named his dog Fred.
5. The man also had a friend_____name was Fred.
6. The dog_____was named Fred came whenever the man called his friend.
7. The friend_____was named Fred came whenever the man called his dog.

8. The moral: People_____want to keep their friends separate from their dogs should not give their dogs human names.

LESSON SEVENTEEN: WRITING SHORT STORIES

The great error in Rip's composition was an insuperable aversion to all kinds of profitable labor. It could not be from the want of assiduity or perseverance; for he would sit on a wet rock, with a rod as long and heavy as a Tartar's lance, and fish all day without a murmur, even though he should not be encouraged by a single nibble. He would carry a fowling piece on his shoulder, for hours together, trudging through woods and swamps, and uphill and down dale, to shoot a few squirrels or wild pigeons. He would never even refuse to assist a neighbor in the roughest toil, and was a foremost man at all country frolics for husking Indian corn, or building stone fences. The women of the village, too, used to employ him to run their errands, and to do such little odd jobs as their less obliging husbands would not do for them; in a word, Rip was ready to attend to anybody's business but his own; but as to doing family duty, and keeping his farm in order, it was impossible.

In fact, he declared it was of no use to work on his farm; it was the most pestilent little piece of ground in the whole country; everything about it went wrong, and would go wrong, in spite of him. His fences were continually falling to pieces; his cow would either go astray or get among the cabbages; weeds were sure to grow quicker in his fields than anywhere else; the rain always made a point of setting in just as he had some outdoor work to do; so that though his patrimonial estate had dwindled away under his management, acre by acre, until there was little more left than a mere patch of Indian corn and potatoes, yet it was the worst-conditioned farm in the neighborhood.

His children, too, were as ragged and wild as if they belonged to nobody. His son Rip, an urchin begotten in his own likeness, promised to inherit the habits, with the old clothes, of his father. He was generally seen trooping like a colt at his mother's heels, equipped in a pair of his father's cast-off galligaskins[7], which he

---

[7] loose fitting trousers worn in the 16th and 17th centuries

had much ado to hold up with one hand, as a fine lady does her train in bad weather.

Rip Van Winkle, however, was one of those happy mortals, of foolish, well-oiled dispositions, who take the world easy, eat white bread or brown, whichever can be got with least thought or trouble, and would rather starve on a penny than work for a pound. If left to himself, he would have whistled life away, in perfect contentment; but his wife kept continually dinning in his ears about his idleness, his carelessness, and the ruin he was bringing on his family. Morning, noon, and night, her tongue was incessantly going, and everything he said or did was sure to produce a torrent of household eloquence. Rip had but one way of replying to all lectures of the kind, and that, by frequent use, had grown into a habit. He shrugged his shoulders, shook his head, cast up his eyes, but said nothing. This, however, always provoked a fresh volley from his wife, so that he was fain to draw off his forces, and take to the outside of the house—the only side which, in truth, belongs to a henpecked husband.

Rip's sole domestic adherent was his dog Wolf, who was as much henpecked as his master; for Dame Van Winkle regarded them as companions in idleness, and even looked upon Wolf with an evil eye, as the cause of his master's so often going astray. True it is, in all points of spirit befitting an honorable dog, he was as courageous an animal as ever scoured the woods—but what courage can withstand the ever-during and all-besetting terrors of a woman's tongue? The moment Wolf entered the house his crest fell, his tail drooped to the ground, or curled between his legs; he sneaked about with a gallows air, casting many a sidelong glance at Dame Van Winkle, and at the least flourish of a broomstick or ladle would fly to the door with yelping precipitation.

Washington Irving, *Rip Van Winkle*

By the time you have completed this lesson, you should be able to do the following:

- Organize several paragraphs on the same topic.
- Write an interesting story of several paragraphs.

The basic elements of narrative paragraphs which were covered in the last lesson provide the basis for writing short stories. A short story sets characters in a particular situation and then resolves the situation in a few pages. Such a story requires good descriptive writing skills because the reader must be able to see and experience the characters and their surroundings. The short story also calls for careful thought and planning. The short story requires careful focus and direction. *What* will the main action of the story be? *Where* will your story take place? *Who* will the main characters be? *How* will you resolve any conflicts in your story? These are questions that must be answered early.

The story will also require a strong opening paragraph. The opening paragraph sets the stage for the short story and usually introduces characters who are important to the plot. The opening paragraph can also reveal the location of the action. Primarily, however, the opening paragraph captures the reader's attention. If the first paragraph is dull, readers will probably not want to finish reading the story.

The topic of the excerpt from Washington Irving's story *Rip Van Winkle* is Rip Van Winkle's refusal to work to support his family. Irving opens with his statement that the chief flaw in Van Winkle's character is that he refuses to do any type of "profitable" work. Then he expands that statement to show that Van Winkle is willing to do those tasks he wants to do—fishing, hunting, assisting his neighbors and participating in games. What he refuses to do is work his farm and even though his wife becomes angry with him and his dog, nothing can change his attitude. These attributes of Van Winkle's are key to rest of the story.

The following passage is modified from an incident in the novel *Les Miserables*. Read this passage carefully. Notice that the opening paragraph tells something about the main character's appearance and personality, and the paragraphs which follow illustrate the traits described in the first paragraph:

> Once upon a time in France there lived a kind old priest named Father Myriel. He was short and a little fat with white hair and gleaming white teeth. Because he laughed and smiled often, he made the people who knew him feel very comfortable. Father Myriel loved God very much, and he loved people, too, and did all that he could to help them.

Father Myriel moved to a small town where he lived in a beautiful palace with his younger sister and an old woman who was the housekeeper. Next door to this palace was a little, ugly building which was used as a hospital. The hospital had a small garden which had not been tended for a long time, and the fruit trees and flowers which grew there were brown and wilted.

One day Father Myriel called for the director of the hospital to come to his palace. "How many patients are there in the hospital?" asked the priest.

"There are twenty-six," answered the director.

The priest thought for a moment and then he said, "This is very wrong. Twenty-six of you live in the hospital while only three of us live here in the palace. I will trade with you; you will live in the palace, and I will live in the hospital."

And so they did; the priest and his sister went to live in the ugly little building. But each night when the priest had finished his work, he went for a walk in the little garden. He enjoyed the stars and the flowers and he talked to God, and he was just as happy there as he had been in his wonderful palace.

The opening paragraph of this passage introduces Father Myriel and defines what sort of a person he is. The paragraphs that follow provide an example of his kindness by explaining that he traded his palace for the hospital and yet was as happy as ever. The *topic* of this passage is *Father Myriel's kindness*, and the *thesis idea* is that *he was a priest who did what he could to help the people around him*. The remainder of this story illustrates this point. What elements of this story are appealing? Is the story interesting enough to make the reader want to finish it?

All of the information included in a short story should direct the reader's attention to the main point. It should never become sidetracked with unimportant details. Everything in the story must lead to the main point.

Short stories may be based on fact or fiction. The subject matter is not nearly so important as proper organization of the material. Without good organization, the short story will not flow well from one idea to the next.

The following passage is an excerpt from *The McAloons: A Horse Called Lightning & A House of Clowns*. In this passage, the author relates a specific series of events related to the arrival of the clowns in the town:

When a large crowd had gathered, a most amazing thing happened. A long pole began rising from the roof of a small white house at the end of the street. The house had been deserted for as long as Joy could remember, and no one had thought to pay it any attention. Now every eye was turned on the little house with the pole rising from its roof. As the crowd watched, a large black umbrella popped out of the top of the pole and opened over the house. The umbrella was covered with huge polka dots in red, yellow, green, blue, and purple.

As soon as the umbrella was in place, the garage door opened, and a shiny black car with the top down drove slowly out and parked in the driveway. Out of the car jumped a clown with a big red nose, orange curly hair, and a little black hat. His huge shoes had turned up toes, and his bright red and yellow pants were short and baggy. The clown smiled and bowed to the crowd. Then he held up a sign that said, "Hello, my name is Funnybone," and he bowed again.

Immediately, a very fat girl clown jumped out of the shiny black car and smiled as she curtsied to the crowd. Her hair was also orange and curly, and her eyelashes were like stiff black fans that batted up and down. Her dress looked like a bright patchwork quilt, and she jumped into the air and clicked her shiny black heels together.

Funnybone held up a second sign that said, "This is my wife, Wishbone."

As the crowd watched, a little boy clown hopped out of the car and began running up and down the driveway blowing a shiny tin horn. By now the crowd was laughing loudly.

Funnybone held up another sign that said, "This is our son, Bonehead."

Finally, a tiny white dog with black spots jumped out of the car. The dog was wearing a little pointed hat of the kind that children wear at birthday parties. He began jumping high into the air and turning flips, and doing all sorts of wonderful tricks.

Funnybone held up a sign that said, "This is our dog, Milkbone."

While all of this was going on, more and more people had called their friends. The business owners had closed their shops and hurried over to join the crowd. Soon everyone in town had gathered on Wild Rose Lane to watch the amazing sight—everyone, that is, except old Mr. Grumpford who was the President of the Bank.

As soon as the bank employees arrived at the little white house on Wild Rose Lane they forgot all about old Mr. Grumpford. The clown family was dancing and squirting each other with water bottles, and the little dog was performing all sorts of tricks.

Joy and Andy laughed until tears rolled down their faces. Mama and Daddy were laughing and enjoying the show too, and they did not notice that Andy had slowly moved forward until he was only a few feet away from Funnybone. Suddenly, Funnybone reached down, picked Andy up and jumped into the shiny black car, setting Andy on the seat beside him. Just as suddenly Wishbone, Bonehead, and their little dog Milkbone jumped into the car with them.

Before Funnybone could drive away, Joy ran forward and snatched Andy from the car. When she picked Andy up, she looked straight into Funnybone's eyes. Joy was surprised to see that they were not happy eyes. Even though Funnybone's mouth was smiling, his eyes looked dark and angry.

Everyone watched as the shiny black car drove back inside the garage and the door closed. The umbrella disappeared into the pole, and the pole sank back into the roof. The music stopped, and everything was quiet.

Joyce Swann, *The McAloons: A Horse Called Lightning*
& A House of Clowns

Reread this story looking for the specific elements which we have discussed in this lesson. What is the topic? What is the thesis idea? How does the author relate this story in such a way that it is interesting to read?

PRACTICE

The exercise below will give you practice in writing a short story. Follow the instructions carefully. Be sure to use detailed description:

Exercise A:

Write a story of between four and five paragraphs about a real or fictional character. In the first paragraph, describe the person's appearance and basic personality. In the second and third paragraphs, relate one incident about that person which illustrates the characteristics you have described. For instance, if you are writing about a person who is basically mean and villainous, in the first paragraph you will describe the appearance of the person and state that this character is wicked. In your other paragraphs you will give an example of one particularly wicked or hateful action of this person. Or, if your character is basically generous, in the first paragraph you will state that the person is very generous and then in your subsequent paragraphs you will describe a generous act by this person. Try to make the opening paragraph as interesting as possible.

Exercise B:

Write a story of between four and five paragraphs in which you relate one incident in the life of a person. It may be something the person did which was brave, humorous, or exciting. Begin by introducing the character in the first paragraph. Then discuss what happened to the person using time order.

GRAMMAR CHECK

Joining Clauses without Connectives

Two related independent clauses—clauses which express similar ideas of equal importance—can be joined without connectives. However, a semi-colon must be used between the clauses. Study the following examples:

The afternoon was dark; the sky was heavy with clouds.

Children need love and attention; without it they do not thrive.

The horses were magnificent creatures; they were the most beautiful he had ever seen.

The Christmas lights danced in the window; they cast a red glow into the night.

Do *not* use a comma where a semi-colon is required. This is called a comma splice and is always incorrect.

Self-Check Test

Join the following independent clauses using a semi-colon. Follow the example:

Example: The weeds had overgrown the dusty road. The truck could hardly pass.

Answer: The weeds had overgrown the dusty road; the truck could hardly pass.

1. Cinderella is a charming children's fairytale. It has been loved for centuries.
2. The story takes place in a kingdom far away. We are never told the specific location.
3. Cinderella is a beautiful girl. She has long blonde hair and huge blue eyes.
4. Her stepsisters are very cruel to her. They are jealous of her beauty.
5. Cinderella has no human friends. Her only companions are mice who live in her house.
6. One day a fairy godmother appears to Cinderella. She gives her a chance to go to a ball.
7. At the ball, a prince sees her. He immediately falls in love.
8. Cinderella and the prince are married. They live happily ever after.

You have now learned several ways of combining clauses to make sentences. You should use all of these methods in your writing. Do not overdo any one method, however.

Occasionally using a semi-colon to combine clauses can make writing sound more forceful. If this is overused, though, the sentences begin to sound choppy and unsophisticated.

Make a conscious effort to vary your writing as much as possible. For example, do not start all of your sentences the same way. Begin some with independent clauses and some with dependent clauses. Do not rely on the same subordinating, adverbial, or coordinating connectives. Try not to use any connective more than once in a paragraph.

Write sentences of varying lengths. Short sentences are very effective in making your writing sound forceful; longer sentences can make your writing smoother and easier to read.

When you finish your writing assignments, read them critically. Look to see if you have used the same sentence pattern or patterns repeatedly or whether all of your sentences are the same length or begin basically the same way. If you find that your writing sounds repetitious, rewrite the assignment to make it more interesting.

WORD CHECK

Using Who and Whom

A previous *Grammar Check* explained that the words *who* and *whom* belong to a special class of pronouns called *relative* pronouns. *Who* and *whom* can also function as a class of pronouns called *interrogative pronouns*. Interrogative pronouns are pronouns that are used to ask questions.

Many times when writers are uncertain of whether to use *who* or *whom* they try to use the word *that* instead. Common expressions include, "The girl *that* won the contest" rather than "the girl *who* won the contest." This is always incorrect. This Word Check is devoted to teaching the difference between *who* and *whom*.

Who is a subject; *whom* is an object. *Whom* may be the object of a preposition or a direct object, but remember that it is always an object pronoun. If *whom* is used as an interrogative pronoun, it will appear before both the subject and the verb. In order to determine whether *who* or *whom* should be used, first determine the subject of the sentence. Study the following examples:

> I have never seen the actor *who* appeared on stage. (*He* appeared on stage.)

> I have never met the girl to *whom* I write. (I have never met *her*.)

> By *whom* was the picnic announcement written? (It was written by *them*.)

> *Who* said the picnic was going to be at the lake? (*She* said it was.)

> *Who* decided I should carry the firewood? (*He* decided I should carry it.)

> You will be reporting to Miss Johnson, *whom* you will see this afternoon. (You will see *her* this afternoon.)

Ignore expressions such as *they know, I think*, or *you think* in determining whether to use *who* or *whom* in a clause:

> *Who* do you believe is the right person to head the committee? (The subject is *who*.)

Self-Check Test

Choose the correct pronoun for each of the following sentences. Remember that the word *whom* is always used after any preposition:

1. (Who/Whom) has the keys to the offices?
2. Do you know (who/whom) has been invited?
3. For (who/whom) is the package?
4. By (who/whom) is the invoice signed?
5. (Who/Whom) is she interviewing?
6. (Who/Whom) ordered the steak?
7. (Who/Whom) is the chairman of the board?
8. (Who/Whom) sent the flowers?
9. (Who/Whom) are they sending to the new branch?
10. (Who/Whom) is getting the new office?

Now write five sentences using *who* correctly and five sentences using *whom* correctly. Follow the examples provided in this lesson as closely as possible.

Be certain to make the *who/whom* distinction in all the writing assigned to you in this course. Refer to this section whenever you need to refresh your memory about when to use these words properly. Get into the habit of using *who* and *whom* in your speech. If you do, the rules for using these two words will become second nature to you, and they will sound as natural to you as the incorrect forms do now.

GRAMMAR CHECK

Past Tense of Verbs

In English, most verbs form their past tense by adding *d* or *ed* to the present tense form of the verb. If the verb ends in *e*, simply add *d* to the present tense form of the verb. If the verb does not end in *e* add *ed*.

Study the following verbs. Each follows the above rule for changing from present tense to past tense:

walk	walked
jump	jumped
reach	reached
hike	hiked
wait	waited
love	loved
need	needed
desire	desired
quiet	quieted

The *perfect tense* of regular verbs is the same as the past tense. (The *perfect tense* is the form of the verb which is used with *have, has,* or *had.*) The *perfect tense* is used to show the continuation of events over a period of time. Study the following sentences and notice the shift from present to past to perfect tense:

Present

Every day, Jeannie *walks* to school, *attends* her classes, *listens* to the lectures, and *returns* home.

Past

Every day last semester, Jeannie *walked* to school, *attended* her classes, *listened* to the lectures, and *returned* home.

Perfect

Each day this year, Jeannie *has walked* to school, *has attended* her classes, *has listened* to the lectures, and *has returned* home.

A few verbs are irregular. These verbs do not follow the rules for changing their tense from present to past or perfect. You must memorize these to use them correctly:

Present	Past	Past Participle
come	came	(have, has, had) come
run	ran	(have, has, had) run
begin	began	(have, has, had) begun
drink	drank	(have, has, had) drunk
ring	rang	(have, has, had) rung
sing	sang	(have, has, had) sung
swim	swam	(have, has, had) swum
bring	brought	(have, has, had) brought
catch	caught	(have, has, had) caught
say	said	(have, has, had) said
sell	sold	(have, has, had) sold
think	thought	(have, has, had) thought
burst	burst	(have, has, had) burst
hit	hit	(have, has, had) hit
do	did	(have, has, had) done
prove	proved	(have, has, had) proven

eat	ate	(have, has, had) eaten
give	gave	(have, has, had) given
go	went	(have, has, had) gone
grow	grew	(have, has, had) grown
know	knew	(have, has, had) known
ride	rode	(have, has, had) ridden
take	took	(have, has, had) taken
write	wrote	(have, has, had) written
break	broke	(have, has, had) broken
choose	chose	(have, has, had) chosen
fly	flew	(have, has, had) flown
freeze	froze	(have, has, had) frozen
speak	spoke	(have, has, had) spoken
tear	tore	(have, has, had) torn
wear	wore	(have, has, had) worn

Self-Check Test

Rewrite the following sentences using the correct form of the verb in parentheses:

1. Yesterday Terri (walk) five miles in the rain without an umbrella.
2. Terri has (walk) in the rain several times in the past.
3. Before he left, Mr. Smith (take) the newspaper.
4. I have (speak) to him about this in the past.
5. The canister will (burst) if you heat it.
6. The speaker has not yet (prove) his points.
7. The book still has to be (write).
8. Because of the accident, she will have to be (take) to the trauma center.
9. The secretary has (run) off copies of the reports.
10. The magazine had (grow) fifty percent by 1985.
11. The manager has (speak) to the employees several times this year.
12. Mr. Hill (write) home several times last year.
13. All of the people on the committee (know) each other when the session began.

14. I always like to (eat) a light snack just before I go to bed.
15. Johnny (eat) the entire cream pie by himself.
16. You have (eat) much more than you should have.
17. I (call) my parents because I knew I would be late.
18. I (call) several times each week if I can afford it.

WORD CHECK

More Misused Words

May/Can

May is used to ask or give permission:

> Mother, *may* I go to the park and spend the afternoon with Tina?

> You *may* open the window if you like.

Can is used to indicate physical ability to complete a task:

> My brother *can* bench press two hundred pounds.

> I *can* run five miles without tiring.

Was/Were

Was is the past tense singular form of the verb *be*. It is used with *he, she*, and *I* or with a singular noun:

> I *was* the head cheerleader when I *was* in school.

> He *was* my fiancé for five years.

> Mary *was* the best cook in the entire community.

Were is the past tense plural form of the verb *be*. *Were* should be used when discussing more than one person and when using the word *you*:

You *were* the best reader in school.

They *were* always very good friends until the night of the accident.

Were is always used with *if*. Never use the phrases *if I was, if he was, if she was*, etc. Use *were* instead. Likewise, the phrase *I wish I was* is always incorrect. The correct phrase is *I wish I were*.

Less/Fewer

Less is singular. Use the word *less* with singular words:

We have *less* money and *less* insurance than we used to.

Riding a bike is *less* tiring than jogging.

Fewer is plural. Use *fewer* with plural words:

The McGregor farm has *fewer* cows, ducks, and chickens than the Henry farm.

I have had *fewer* headaches since I started taking aspirin.

Between/Among

Between is used when *two* objects, persons, or items are being discussed:

Just *between* you and me, I am a little nervous about taking finals.

The pesky little dog kept running *between* my legs.

We will divide the cake *between* Rebecca and Arthur.

Among is used when *more than two* objects, persons, or items are being discussed:

The United States is a great power *among* the nations of the world.

Among the four of us we should be able to get a nice gift.

Divide the pie *among* the six children.

Self-Check Test

Choose the correct word to complete each sentence:

1. I have (less/fewer) money than Joe.
2. Mark got (less/fewer) questions right than Bob did.
3. You are (between/among) friends.
4. Stand (between/among) Sharon and Mike.
5. (May/Can) we leave?
6. The baby (may/can) talk.
7. He (was/were) the life of the party.
8. She (was/were) as tall as a tree.
9. Mother said I (may/can) stay out late.
10. You (may not/cannot) dance on the table.
11. My brother was somewhere (between/among) the people at the party.
12. Shannon has (less/fewer) fever than she did last night.
13. The child has (less/fewer) marbles since he lost some.
14. Terry (was/were) my best friend.
15. Both of the people (was/were) in an accident.

WORD CHECK

Using the Word *Like*

Like may well be both the most overused and misused word in the English language. The guidelines below will explain when and when not to use this word:

Like should not be used in place of *as* or *as if*. *Like* should never be used to begin a clause. Use *as, as if,* or *as though*:

Incorrect:

He looks *like* he might start crying at any moment.

Correct:

He looks *as though* he might start crying at any moment.

Incorrect:

She looked *like* she had seen a ghost.

Correct:

She looked *as though* she had seen a ghost.

The word *like* is used to show that a person or thing resembles another person or thing. It is used for comparison:

He looks *like* his father.

She looks *like* her aunt.

Like should not be used in place of *such as*:

Incorrect:

Many controversial issues, *like* immigration, divide our nation.

Correct:

Many controversial issues, *such as* immigration, divide our nation.

The expression *like for instance* should never be used:

Incorrect:

Many controversial issues, *like for instance* immigration, divide our country.

Correct:

> Many controversial issues—*for instance,* immigration—divide our country.

Self-Check Test

Read the following sentences carefully. If the word *like* is used correctly, mark a C after the sentence to indicate correct usage. If the word is not used correctly, rewrite the sentence to make it correct:

1. Many people, like for instance my parents, are the children of immigrants.
2. Some of us, like the Irish, came here many years ago.
3. People told my family for years that we looked like we might be from Ireland.
4. Actually, I have been told that I look something like my father, who looks like an Irishman.
5. My friend Sally looks like her mother, and her mother looks like she might be Polish.
6. Other groups, like the Russians, came to America at the turn of the century.
7. It is interesting to see pictures of family members from like another country.
8. My family has some friends who look very much like their cousins from Germany.
9. Watching the different branches of the family together is like looking at my friends in a mirror.
10. It is like they are one big family from overseas.

UNIT TEST

PART I: Choosing the Correct Word

Underline the correct word in each sentence:

1. (Beside/Besides) the door stood the young man.
2. I cannot go to work today; (beside/besides) I do not really want to be there.
3. The frightened child ran (in/into) his mother's arms.
4. Use the water (in/into) the sink to wash the dishes.
5. (Here/Hear) are the reasons for our decision.
6. I can (hear/here) every word they say.
7. The (affect/effect) of the report was very detrimental.
8. This has (affected/effected) everyone in the organization.

PART II: Using Who and Whom

Read the following sentences carefully. If the pronouns are used properly, write a C after each sentence. If not, rewrite the sentences to make them correct:

1. The man whom is the supervisor is my brother.
2. Who are you going to call?
3. The flowers are for who?
4. Who is here?
5. Who do you trust?
6. Jack, who you will meet in the morning, is very friendly.
7. Tracy, who is going to arrive this evening, will be the new accountant.
8. Who did the people elect as mayor?
9. Nelson, who is turning five, wants a red balloon for his birthday.
10. Of the three candidates, who do you think is best qualified?

PART III: Joining Sentences without Connectives

Join the following sentences without connectives. Punctuate carefully:

1. *The Man in the Iron Mask* is a great book. I have read it several times.
2. Jeff is the lead basketball player. He is also the tallest person here.
3. Christy liked roses very much. This year she planted several rose bushes.
4. Rosie seems to have the perfect life. She has a great job and a wonderful husband.
5. He who laughs last laughs best. You should be laughing for the rest of your life.

PART IV: Using Words Properly

Read each of the following sentences. If the italicized word is used properly, write a C after the sentence. If the word is used incorrectly, substitute the correct word:

1. John has had *less* opportunities than Mary.
2. Mary *can* stay out until ten P.M. if she calls us.
3. I *may* start an exercise program now since I am physically strong enough.
4. I *may* start an exercise program if my doctor gives me permission.
5. *Fewer* than fifty people will qualify for the scholarship.
6. He looks *like* he is having a bad day.
7. The child looks *like* his mother.
8. I have a lot of questions about the job, *like for instance*, how far I will have to commute to work.

PART V: Essay

Write a short story of three-to-five typed, double-spaced pages. Focus your story on one incident taking place over one afternoon in the life of one character. Relate the circumstances in such a way that by the end of the story, the reader will have some insight into the personality of the character you have created. You will probably find that the most difficult part of this assignment will be actually limiting yourself to five pages, but it is important to follow this guideline so that you will remain focused on your goal of relating one specific incident.

When you have finished your story, read it aloud to yourself and make whatever editing changes you believe to be necessary. When you have finished, give the story to a friend, and let that person make suggestions.

If you are using this course with a group of people, plan a time to get together and share your stories. Allow the group to provide some additional ideas for each story.

Next to doing things that deserve to be written, there is nothing that gets a man more credit or gives him more pleasure, than to write things that deserve to be read.

LORD CHESTERFIELD, *LETTERS* (1739)

UNIT FOUR

Writing that Shows Relationship

LESSON EIGHTEEN: USING CAUSE AND EFFECT

There seemed to be no use in waiting by the little door, so she went back to the table, half hoping she might find another key on it, or at any rate a book of rules for shutting people up like telescopes: this time she found a little bottle on it ("which certainly was not here before," said Alice), and tied round the neck of the bottle was a paper label with the words "**DRINK ME**" beautifully printed on it in large letters.

It was all very well to say "Drink me," but the wise little Alice was not going to do that in a hurry. "No, I'll look first," she said, "and see whether it's marked 'poison' or not," for she had read several nice little stories about children who had got burnt, and eaten up by wild beasts, and other unpleasant things, all because they would not remember the simple rules their friends had taught them, such as that a red-hot poker will burn you if you hold it too long; and that if you cut your finger very deeply with a knife it usually bleeds; and she had never forgotten that if you drink from a bottle marked "poison," it is almost certain to disagree with you sooner or later.

However, this bottle was not marked "poison," so Alice ventured to taste it, and finding it very nice (it had, in fact, a sort of mixed flavor of cherry tart, custard, pineapple, roast turkey, toffy, and hot buttered toast), she very soon finished it off.

"What a curious feeling!" said Alice. "I must be shutting up like a telescope."

And so it was, indeed; she was now only ten inches high, and her face brightened up at the thought that she was now the right size for going through the little door into that lovely garden.

Lewis Carroll, *Alice's Adventures in Wonderland*

By the time you have completed this lesson, you should be able to do the following:

- Understand the relationship between causes and effects in your writing.
- Construct effective sentences demonstrating cause and effect.

Writing that shows a relationship between one event and another event which takes place as a result of the first event is called *cause and effect* writing. The *cause* is the action or event which makes another event occur. The event which takes place as a result of the cause is called the *effect*. The cause is usually the first event in a series of circumstances—an event which results in other events taking place. Transition words such as *therefore, as a result,* and *consequently* are used to signal the transition from cause to effect.

In cause and effect writing, at least two events take place. The cause is the first event to happen in natural time order. The effect takes place *after* the cause. Study the following cause and effect sentences. In each sentence, the cause is italicized, and the effect is in bold type:

Because *the cat tripped me*, **I dropped the vase.**

The terrible rain storm tore out the power lines, and **we went without electricity for two days.**

I have had terrible back problems since *I was in a car accident six months ago.*

My Uncle Bob died *after a serious heart attack.*

In each of the above sentences, the cause is the first event which occurred in natural time order, and as a result, something else took place. In the first sentence, *the cat tripped me* before *I dropped the vase.* If the cat had not tripped me, I would not have dropped the vase. Therefore, this event is the cause of the vase being dropped.

In the second sentence there are a series of cause and effect relationships. *First,* the rainstorm occurred—this caused the power lines to be torn out; *then,* the power lines being torn out caused us to go without power.

Notice that sentences three and four are written in inverted order—the cause is not the first event in the sentence order, although it is the first event which occurred. In the third sentence, I was in a serious car accident *before* I began experiencing back trouble. The accident was the cause of my back problems. In the fourth sentence, my Uncle Bob had a heart attack *first* which resulted in his death.

Sometimes one cause has many effects, several causes have one effect, or several causes have several effects. In the following examples, the events which cause the other events are italicized; the effects appear in bold:

> *When Jared lost control of the car,* **it spun around twice, skidded off the road, and slammed into a tree.**

> *When you put off studying, stay out late, and party all night,* **it is hard to pass a test the next day.**

> People who *eat fresh fruits and vegetables, drink lots of water, and get good exercise* **look better, feel better, and are generally healthier than those who do not.**

PRACTICE

The exercises below will test your understanding of the cause and effect relationship:

Exercise A:

Underline the cause once and the effect twice in each of the following sentences:

1. If you develop a habit of gambling, you will eventually lose everything you own.
2. The baby began crying when the ambulance sped screaming past the house.
3. The frightened cat ran up the tree when the snarling dog came charging from the barn.

4. The cold, wet wind hit the boys chilling them to the bone and causing them to catch cold.
5. Since the child was small and wiry, he could easily crawl through the large air-conditioning ducts of the abandoned office building.

Exercise B:

Write ten cause and effect sentences of your own. Then underline the cause and circle the effect in each sentence.

PUNCTUATION CHECK

Using Commas

Use a comma after any *introductory modifier* of more than three words. An introductory modifier is a group of words which tells *when* or *how* something was done:

> *Before beginning to eat,* we said grace.
>
> *After winning the championship*, John threw a party.
>
> *On Tuesdays and Thursdays*, I get up early.

Use a comma to set off any verbal or verbal phrase at the beginning of a sentence. (*Verbals* are verb forms such as *writing, looking, to look, looked,* etc. which have taken on the role of other sentence parts.) The *verbal phrase* is the verbal and the other material it contains:

> *To get to work on time,* we have to leave very early.
>
> *Laughing*, he walked out the door.

Use a comma to set off familiar expressions such as: *of course, however, unfortunately, consequently, on the other hand, in addition, certainly,* and *surely.* If the expression appears at the beginning of the sentence, use the comma after it. If it appears at the end of the sentence, use a comma before it. If it appears in the middle of the sentence, use a comma before and after it:

Of course, I will be there before you arrive.

The paper was so vague that, *unfortunately,* it could be easily misinterpreted.

Self-Check Test

Exercise A:

Use commas where necessary in the following sentences. Check your answers with the answer key:

1. To arrive at the airport before the flight we had to leave in the morning.
2. My brother to name one individual was totally opposed to the new restrictions.
3. Howard Smith on the other hand liked every idea the company had.
4. To obtain all the information we had to search through many reports.
5. In the end however we found what we needed.
6. During the entire process I never lost faith.
7. Before the meeting ended we were able to present our findings.
8. Delighted with the results we left the meeting and returned to work.
9. Before the day was out the changes we recommended had been approved.
10. In spite of the difficulties we accomplished our goals.

Exercise B:

Now write ten sentences of your own using each of the rules presented in this lesson as a guide. Be sure to use the proper punctuation in each sentence.

Review your last paragraph against the comma rules you have finished studying. Did you omit commas where they should have been used? Did you use commas where you should not have? Rewrite the paragraph using the guidelines you have learned for punctuating with commas.

PUNCTUATION CHECK

Commas with Relative and Noun Clauses

A *restrictive clause* is a relative clause which identifies a noun. Because restrictive clauses are considered essential to the meaning of the sentence, they should not be followed by a comma. Study the following example:

> The girl *who sat next to me in class* was my best friend.

(The other girls in the class were not my best friends. The clause distinguishes this girl from the others.)

> The boys *who played basketball* were very popular.

(The other boys were not so popular.)

When the relative clause is used with a noun that has already been identified, the clause is usually *non-restrictive*. Although the clause gives extra information about the noun, it does not change the meaning of the sentence. Study the difference in meaning between these two pairs of sentences:

> I called to the man *who was crossing the street*. (The clause identifies the man.)

> I called to my father, *who was crossing the street*. (This clause does not identify who the man is; I have already stated that he is my father. The clause merely tells what my father was doing when I called to him.)

> The girl *who was acting as the lifeguard* saved the child. (Identifies the girl)

> Helen Grady, *who was acting as the lifeguard*, saved the child. (Tells what Helen was doing at the time)

Notice that when the clause is positioned in the middle of the sentence, as in the second example above, the comma appears before and after it.

When *that* is used to begin a relative clause, the clause is usually essential to the meaning of the sentence and, therefore, restrictive. Do not use the comma:

> Cars *that do not belong to customers* will be towed.
>
> Many buildings *that were built in the nineteenth century* are still standing.
>
> Dogs *that live in houses* are usually spoiled.
>
> The cat *that the neighbors owned* was white with blue eyes.

Sometimes we leave the word *that* out of the clause. The punctuation remains the same:

> Dogs *in houses* are usually spoiled.
>
> The cat *the neighbors owned* was white with blue eyes.
>
> Many buildings *built in the nineteenth century* are still standing.

Self-Check Test

Exercise A:

Punctuate the following sentences by adding commas where they belong. Some of the sentences require no punctuation:

1. The child who lived next door was very sweet.
2. His mother who worked all day used to ask me to baby-sit for him.
3. They had a black Great Dane named Spot.
4. He was the biggest dog that I had ever seen.
5. Spot would bite even though Mrs. Marks said he would not.
6. He once bit a postal worker who was trying to deliver a letter.
7. I was not afraid of Spot though I knew that the other children in the neighborhood were.

8. My mother who was frightened of dogs used to ask me why I was not afraid.
9. I knew that Spot would not bite me.
10. Spot did everything that Eric who was Mrs. Marks' older son said.

Exercise B:

Practice punctuating relative and noun clauses properly in your own writing. When you have completed the next writing assignment, reread your paragraph looking for relative clauses. Circle each clause you have used. Then, look to see whether each relative clause is restrictive or non-restrictive. If the clause is non-restrictive, set it off with commas. If the clause is restrictive, do not use the commas.

LESSON NINETEEN: CAUSE AND EFFECT PARAGRAPHS

A merchant had done good business at the fair. He had sold his wares and filled his bag with gold and silver. Then he set out at once on his journey home, for he wished to be in his own house before night.

At noon he rested in a town. When he wanted to go on, the stable boy brought his horse saying, "A nail is wanting, sir, in the shoe of his left hind foot."

"Let it be wanting," answered the merchant, "the shoe will stay on for the six miles I have yet to go. I am in a hurry."

In the afternoon he got down at an inn and had his horse fed. The stable boy came into the room and said, "Sir, a shoe is wanting from your horse's left hind foot. Shall I take him to the blacksmith?"

"Let it still be wanting," said the man: "the horse can very well hold out for two or three miles more. I am in a hurry."

So he merchant rode forth, but before long the horse began to limp. The horse had not limped very long before he began to stumble, and he had not stumbled long before he fell down and broke his leg. The merchant had to leave the horse where he fell, and unstrap the bag, take it on his back, and go home on foot.

"That unlucky nail," said he to himself, "has made all this trouble."

Jacob and Wilhelm Grimm, *The Grimm's Fairy Tales*

By the time you have completed this lesson, you should be able to do the following:

- Understand how to design cause and effect paragraphs.
- Construct cause and effect paragraphs of your own.

Now that we have studied cause and effect sentences, writing cause and effect paragraphs will be easy. Cause and effect paragraphs may be organized in three ways: *cause paragraphs, effect paragraphs*, or *a combination of the two*.

A cause paragraph will consist mostly of causes—events which caused something else to take place. The paragraph will contain one effect, or result, of these other events. Study the following example:

> I was twenty minutes late for work yesterday, and my employer was really angry. My problems began when I overslept five minutes. That alone really would not have made me late, but I soon discovered that all my shirts were wrinkled, and I had to iron one. This cost me another five minutes. I was now ten minutes late, though I was confident that I could make up the lost time on the freeway. In spite of my earlier problems, I probably would have arrived at the office on time if I had not encountered the traffic jam that delayed me for another twenty minutes and caused me so much trouble.

In the above paragraph, several causes are listed, all of which give reasons explaining why the author was late for work. The fact that he was late is the sole effect listed in the paragraph. In this paragraph, the one effect is mentioned first, and after it are listed several causes which contributed to that event. Putting the effect first is an example of inverted order in a cause and effect paragraph.

Effect paragraphs consist of several effects which occur as a result of one cause. These, too, can be written in normal order with the cause being listed first and the effects following. They can also be inverted so that the effects appear first and the cause is mentioned last. Study the following example of an effect paragraph:

> As soon as night falls on Halloween, all of the pranksters in my neighborhood come out. Although people have thrown eggs on my car and my house, I consider myself one of the lucky ones. Last year someone filled Mr. Andrews' mailbox with shaving cream and wrapped neon warning tape on all of his trees. Another prankster gave Mrs. Davis' dog a haircut, while still another painted, "Happy Halloween" with weed killer on my friend Mark's front lawn. In my neighborhood, the night is a nightmare.

In the above paragraph, the cause is stated first and then all of the effects are described. This type of paragraph is relatively simple to write.

Though they are a little more difficult to create, some paragraphs combine cause and effect sentences throughout the paragraph. Almost every pair of sentences states a cause and an effect. Study the following example:

> Waitressing at my sister's café last weekend was quite an experience. Because one of my sister's waitresses was ill, I volunteered to take her place. Little did I know what was in store for me. I got the orders to the cook on time, but I could not seem to get the food to the proper tables because I could not remember what each patron had ordered. In my eagerness to serve the customers quickly, I picked up a hot bowl. In agony and surprise, I dropped it! Soup splashed across the floor. Fellow waitresses went slipping and sliding across the kitchen. After a day of being pushed, bumped, burned, and threatened by the customers and the cook, I was tired and cranky. Still, I kept smiling and hoping to get a tip. Finally, I received one from a kindly old gentleman who said he liked my smile so much that he did not even mind the fact that I had served him someone else's roast beef dinner.

PRACTICE

Exercise A:

Below are two cause and two effect sentences. First, study each sentence carefully to determine whether it states a cause or an effect. Then write five or six supporting sentences to create a paragraph for each:

1. Julie has the nicest hair in our school.
2. I have recently taken up jogging.
3. The tornado which tore through Midland, Texas, last week destroyed much of the city.
4. I sprained my knee in a skiing accident last January.

Exercise B:

Write a combination cause and effect paragraph based on an event which has happened to you recently. For instance, you might write about your first morning on a new job or babysitting your little sister. Choose a topic that is not too broad and that can be discussed well in one paragraph. Be sure that your paragraph shows a series of cause and effect events.

WORD CHECK

Expressions to Avoid

Do not use the expressions *being as, being that, seeing as how*, or *on account of* in formal writing. Each of these informal expressions has the same general meaning as *because* or *since*. Substitute the more formal wording for each of these expressions:

Incorrect:

   Seeing as how you need help, let me give you some advice.

Correct:

   Because you need help, I will give you some advice.

Do not use *without* or *on account of* to start a clause with its own subject and verb. Use *unless* instead of *without* and *because* instead of *on account of:*

Incorrect:

   We will never hear from him *without* we call.

Correct:

   We will never hear from him *unless* we call.

Incorrect:

I will do it *on account of* he needs help.

Correct:

I will do it *because* he needs help.

Do not use *learned me* rather than *taught me.*

Incorrect:

Mother *learned me* how to do the dishes.

Correct:

Mother *taught me* how to do the dishes.

Do not use *nowheres, somewheres,* or *nohow.* The correct expressions are *nowhere, somewhere, not at all,* or *anyhow:*

Incorrect:

The papers are *nowheres* to be found.

Correct:

The papers are *nowhere* to be found.

Incorrect:

He is around here *somewheres.*

Correct:

He is around here *somewhere.*

Do not use *the reason is because*. The correct expression is *the reason is that:*

Incorrect:

The *reason* he left *is because* he had to go to work.

Correct:

The *reason* he left *is that* he had to go to work.

Self-Check Test

Rewrite the following sentences using formal English. Substitute the correct phrase for the non-standard phrase which appears in the sentence:

1. Being that he is my brother, I will give him a loan.
2. I agreed to go to the party on account of you were going to be there.
3. Seeing as how the dog likes me, I will let him stay.
4. I won't go to the doctor without you agree to come with me.
5. At school my teachers learned me how to write.
6. He is not going to go to medical school nohow.
7. Somewheres around here is my brother's address.
8. The reason they wrote the letter is because they wanted to give us the new address.
9. Being as this is my house, I can do what I like.
10. I will never speak to you again without you apologize.

PUNCTUATION CHECK

More Practice with Commas

As previous lessons have demonstrated, a clause that provides information essential to the meaning of the sentence is called a restrictive clause. A comma should not be used when the dependent clause at the end of the sentence is restrictive. For example, the statement, "You may take the car on Sunday," has a

159

different meaning from, "You may take the car on Sunday if you agree to put gas in it." The clause at the end has created a condition under which I will allow you to drive the car. This condition was not present in the first sentence. Similarly, the sentence, "I talked to the man," differs from the sentence, "I talked to the man who was in charge of the project." In the first sentence I do not specify to whom I spoke; in the second sentence the clause makes the identity of the person clear.

Use a comma when the dependent clause at the end of the sentence is *non-restrictive*. A non-restrictive clause is one which does not change the meaning of the sentence. Study the following examples:

Non-Restrictive:

> I do not speak French, *although I lived in France for many years.*

> Americans celebrate the Fourth of July, *whereas the British celebrate the queen's birthday.*

> William Jennings Bryant never became president, *though he ran several times.*

Restrictive:

> I will not participate in the project *unless you agree to help me.*

> The banks will be closed *if this is a federal holiday.*

> You should continue to see the doctor *until you make a full recovery.*

Remember to use a comma when the dependent clause begins the sentence.

Self-Check Test

Insert commas where necessary in the following sentences. If the sentence does not require a comma, write No Comma after it:

1. John may come with us if he gets here in time.
2. There is no way we can finish by Tuesday no matter what Mr. Davidson says.
3. My dad will loan me the money for school if I cannot get it myself.
4. The door was locked even though Jane said it was open.
5. The truck broke down while we were on the freeway.
6. Before I won the championship everyone told me I had no chance.
7. She promised to do whatever she could to help if we needed her.
8. The school will be open Thursday unless it snows.
9. I have always supported your decisions even when I did not agree with you.
10. If you marry for money you will always be miserable.

LESSON TWENTY: COMPARISON AND CONTRAST

It was the best of times, it was the worst of times, it was the age of wisdom, it was the age of foolishness, it was the epoch of belief, it was the epoch of incredulity, it was the season of Light, it was the season of Darkness, it was the spring of hope, it was the winter of despair, we had everything before us, we had nothing before us, we were all going direct to Heaven, we were all going direct the other way—in short, the period was so far like the present period that some of its noisiest authorities insisted on its being received, for good or for evil, in the superlative degree of comparison only.

Charles Dickens, *A Tale of Two Cities*

To *compare* two objects is to show the ways in which they are similar. To *contrast* two objects is to show the ways in which they are different. Thus, *comparison paragraphs* are paragraphs which emphasize the ways in which two people, objects, or ideas are alike while *contrast paragraphs* emphasize the ways in which they are different.

One of the most famous pieces of comparison/contrast is found in the book of Ecclesiastes:

To every thing there is a season, and a time to every purpose under the heaven:

A time to be born, and a time to die; a time to plant, and a time to pluck up that which is planted;

A time to kill, and a time to heal; a time to break down, and a time to build up;

A time to weep, and a time to laugh; a time to mourn, and a time to dance;

A time to cast away stones, and a time to gather stones together; a time to embrace, and a time to refrain from embracing;

A time to get, and a time to lose; a time to keep, and a time to cast away;

A time to rend[8], and a time to sew; a time to keep silence, and a time to speak;

A time to love, and a time to hate; a time of war, and a time of peace.

Ecclesiastes 3: 1-8

By the time you have completed this lesson, you should be able to do the following:

- Understand comparison and contrast.
- Incorporate comparison and contrast into your writing.

Often when we speak of comparing two things, we are really talking about both comparing and contrasting them. Most assignments which ask for a comparison of ideas or individuals will really require a discussion of both the similarities and the differences.

There are two specific styles of comparative writing. In the first style, the similarities or differences between two subjects are broken down *point-by-point*. When writing about the similarities between two objects, one feature of the first subject is immediately compared with the corresponding feature of the second subject. Thus, what they have in common is highlighted *point-by-point*. Study the following *point-by-point* paragraph contrasting a horse and a donkey. Notice that as each feature of the horse is mentioned, it is immediately contrasted with a corresponding feature of the donkey:

---

[8] tear

A horse and a donkey are quite different. A horse is a tall (14-16 hands high), slender animal with long legs, a long face, and comparatively short ears. A donkey, by comparison, is a rather short animal (8-10 hands high) with short legs, a shorter face and proportionately long, wide ears. A horse has tremendous speed and grace while a donkey has enormous endurance and surprising strength for its small size. Moreover, horses can be found in a variety of colors ranging from black to white, in varying shades of grays, reds, creams and browns; they may be speckled, spotted, blotched, or marked in just about every conceivable way. Donkeys, on the other hand, are relatively consistent in their markings around the muzzles, legs, and stomachs and are usually brown, black, or gray.

The second style of comparative writing is known as *block style*. In this style, all of the information about the first subject is presented at one time. Then, all of the contrasting information about the other subject is presented in a second block. In the block style, each subject is allowed its own paragraph. Of course, when you write a comparative essay in block style, you must still be certain to compare or contrast the same points in both of your subjects. The following two paragraphs are the horse and donkey paragraph rewritten in this new style. Notice that although the format has changed, the points being contrasted remain the same:

A horse and a donkey are quite different. A horse is a tall, slender animal (14-16 hands high) with long legs, a long face, and comparatively short ears. A horse has tremendous speed and grace. Moreover, horses can be found in a variety of colors ranging from black to white, in varying shades of grays, reds, creams and browns; they can be speckled, spotted, blotched, and marked in just about every conceivable way.

A donkey, by comparison, is a rather short animal (8-10 hands high) with short legs, a shorter face and proportionately long, wide ears. A donkey has enormous endurance and surprising strength for its small size. Unlike horses, donkeys are relatively consistent in their markings around the muzzle, legs, and stomach and are usually brown, black or gray.

The block style is used most effectively in contrasting two subjects. It may not work well for making comparisons. A comparison should include both subjects and utilize the point-by-point style. The following is an example of a comparison paragraph written in point-by-point style:

> German Shepherds and Rottweilers have many similarities. Both originally came to America from Germany, and both were once used to guard sheep and properties in their native land. Both German Shepherds and Rottweilers are large dogs with strong body builds, sharp eyesight, and a keen sense of smell. These traits have made both animals ideal for working with police, drug traffic, and border patrol officers. Moreover, despite their large size and intimidating appearance, both German Shepherds and Rottweilers are even-tempered and have proven to be good pets for children with whom they are raised.

Of course, comparisons may involve several paragraphs. The first paragraph might be devoted to one subject and the second to the other. Then the comparison is made in a later paragraph. Study the following tongue-in-cheek comparison of Pontius Pilate and Santa Claus by Mark Twain:

> In the course of the morning we passed the spot where Pontius Pilate is said to have thrown himself into the lake. The legend goes that after the Crucifixion his conscience troubled him, and he fled from Jerusalem and wandered about the earth, weary of life and a prey to tortures of the mind. Eventually, he hid himself away, on the heights of Mount Pilatus, and dwelt alone among the clouds and crags for years; but rest and peace were still denied him, so he finally put an end to his misery by drowning himself.
>
> Presently we passed the place where a man of better odor was born. This was the children's friend, Santa Claus, or St. Nicholas. There are some unaccountable reputations in the world. This saint's is an instance. He has ranked for ages as the peculiar friend of children, yet it appears he was not much of a friend to his own. He had ten of them, and when fifty years old he left them, and sought out as dismal a refuge from the world as possible, and became a hermit in order that he might reflect upon pious themes without being

disturbed by the joyous and other noises from the nursery, doubtless.

Judging by Pilate and St. Nicholas, there exists no rule for the construction of hermits; they seem made out of all kinds of material. But Pilate attended to the matter of expiating his sin while he was alive, whereas St. Nicholas will probably have to go on climbing down sooty chimneys, Christmas Eve, forever, and conferring kindness on other people's children to make up for deserting his own.

Mark Twain, *A Tramp Abroad*

PRACTICE

Listed below are a number of topics for paragraphs. Choose *two* topics; write one as a comparison paragraph and one as a contrast paragraph. Create a topic sentence based on the topic, and then write a paragraph to support that sentence. Your contrast paragraph should be written in block style, while your comparison paragraph should be written in point-by-point style:

TOPICS

The summer and winter weather in your part of the country

Two pets you have owned

You and a family member

Two jobs you have held

High school and college students

LESSON TWENTY-ONE: EXPOSITORY PARAGRAPHS

Davy Crockett was one of the most famous of the frontiersman. From his youth, Davy was fascinated by the wild and unsettled areas of what is now the Southern United States, and at an early age he began exploring new lands on which to settle with his family.

One morning Davy and three neighbors decided to venture out to explore the territory. At night when the men had stopped to rest, their horses broke loose and ran off into the darkness. The next day, Davy took his rifle and chased the horses on foot for about fifty miles. By the end of the day, he was exhausted, but he had still not caught the horses. Tired and discouraged, he stopped at a house along the road for the night.

The next morning when Davy woke, he was very ill. His head was pounding. In spite of that, he set out again and tried to rejoin the other men, but soon he was too sick to walk. Some Native Americans who were passing by helped him get to a nearby house where he spent the night. The next day, these friends took him to the home of Jesse Jones.

Davy was so ill that he nearly died, but after a time he began to recover. A few weeks later he was able to start home. A man who lived close by agreed to transport Davy back to the Crockett house. But when, after so many weeks of being away, Davy finally arrived at his home, his family was very surprised to see him. The neighbors who had started out with Davy on his trip were so certain that he was dead that they had told his family that he had died and that they had spoken to the men who had buried him. When his family told Davy this story, he exclaimed: "I know'd this was a whopper of a lie the minute I heard it!"

By the time you have completed this lesson, you should be able to do the following:

- Understand the principles of expository writing.
- Write clear, informative process paragraphs.

Paragraphs that give information or explanation are called *expository paragraphs*. Newspapers that give basic facts and figures about sports, political issues, weather, and daily events are examples of expository writing. Other examples of expository writing include dictionaries, encyclopedias, almanacs, how-to books, and textbooks. Most of the essays which are assigned in colleges and universities call for expository writing. All give basic information to the reader.

Study the following example of expository writing. This paragraph is an excerpt from a passage about the life of William Cody. Notice that the writer provides specific information about where William Cody was born, the date of his birth, and the town in which he was raised:

> William Frederick Cody, one of the best-known of all Pony Express riders, was born in Scott County, Iowa on February 26, 1846. William was the oldest of seven children. His family moved many times during his childhood. They lived in LeClair, Iowa, and Weston, Missouri, and later moved to a homestead in the Salt Creek Valley near Leavenworth, Kansas.

The writer of this paragraph intended to provide her readers with specific information about William Cody. Notice that each sentence in the paragraph gives real information about Cody—there are no wasted words. Expository writing should be succinct—the sentences should say as much as possible in as few words as possible.

Expository writing can also include writing that explains the process of accomplishing a task. The following paragraph explains how to bake a chocolate cake. Notice that the writer includes each step in the order in which it must be followed:

> Baking a chocolate cake is easy and a lot of fun. **First**, set ¼ cup of butter out on the counter an hour before you are ready to begin so

that it can soften. **Then** butter and lightly flour two eight-inch cake pans. **Next** set the oven at 350 degrees. With a mixer set on low speed, cream the butter and slowly add 1 ½ cups of sugar. Beat until fluffy. **Now**, add three eggs, beating them into the butter/sugar mixture. Blend well. **Next**, add 1 cup of unsweetened cocoa. Measure 1 ¾ cups sifted flour, 2 teaspoons of double-acting baking powder and ½ teaspoon of salt. Add this to the mixture. Add 1 teaspoon of vanilla. **Finally**, pour the batter into the cake pans, and bake for 30 minutes.

In all expository writing, it is important to keep the information in order. What would happen in the paragraph above it the writer gave all of the same information about baking a chocolate cake but did not put the steps in the correct order? Obviously, the recipe would not turn out! Likewise, an essay for a history class might include all of the events surrounding the Boston Massacre, but if the events are not in the correct order, the readers will not be able to understand what happened. Even if all of the information is correct, if it is presented out of order, the subject matter either loses its significance or becomes useless. Always start with the events which took place first, or the steps which should come first, and work consistently to the event or step which is last or most recent.

Transitions link one event to the next. *Transitions* are words which provide a bridge to move the reader from one idea or concept to another. Words that can be used as transitions include: **first, second, third, next, then, before, after, once, when, while, last, and finally.** These help the reader keep the information being presented in order. In the paragraph describing the steps of baking a cake, the transitions appear in boldface type. Reread the paragraph without the transitions. Do the transitions make this paragraph easier to read?

Other words which may be used as transitions appear in **Figure H**:

in addition	moreover	therefore	besides
consequently	meanwhile	furthermore	nevertheless
as a result			

Figure H

Study the following paragraph about the demise of the Pony Express. Notice that the author has not used many transitions, but all the transitions lead the reader from one point to the next. The words used as transitions appear in boldface type:

> The collapse of the Pony Express resulted in bankruptcy for the partners. They had invested $500,000 in the Express and had lost money steadily on the stagecoach line. Russell became so desperate that he even became involved in an embezzlement scheme with a clerk in the Interior Department—a venture which resulted in Russell's being sent to prison. **Ironically**, the firm slid into bankruptcy just as the one chance to secure a government contract presented itself. Because of the outbreak of the Civil War, Congress was forced to move the overland mail service north. **Unfortunately**, the company had been so discredited that it could not be considered. **Instead**, the Butterfield Overland Mail was moved to the central route and awarded the $1,000,000 annual subsidy that Russell, Majors and Waddell had tried so desperately to secure.

PRACTICE

Exercise A:

This exercise tests your understanding of transitions. Combine the following blocks of sentences using the transitions listed in the chart which is part of the exercise. Be sure to choose transitions which are appropriate to the sentences. Punctuate properly using the rules you learned in the Punctuation Check. The example has been done for you:

Example: John wanted money for a new car. He took an extra job.

Answer: John wanted money for a new car; *therefore*, he took an extra job.

therefore	moreover	however	furthermore	
nevertheless	in fact	as a result	notwithstanding	then

1. John wanted money for a new car. He refused to go to work.
2. Mark and Cindy were best friends. They spent all of their time together.
3. The little tree grew up in the scorching hot sun without any shade. In the summer it died.
4. Philip never studied in high school. He spent all of his time with his friends.
5. Philip never studied in high school. He failed every course.
6. Being president of the United States is a very demanding job. It is also very rewarding.
7. To get to my house, go to Scott Street and turn right. Take a left at the stop light.
8. A knowledge of history can be very important. It can help you in many professions.
9. Vicious dogs can be dangerous. They should be confined to their own yards.
10. People have the right to vote. They should take a greater part in the government.

Exercise B:

Choose ONE of the following topics. In two well-written paragraphs, discuss step-by-step how to do what the topic requires. Start with a good topic sentence. You may use the suggested topic sentences which appear across from each paragraph topic. Be sure to develop your topic properly, and make good use of transitions.

Topics	*Suggested topic sentence*
How to cook hamburgers	Cooking hamburgers is fun and easy.
How to be a good baby-sitter	Being a good baby-sitter requires patience.
How to dive safely into a swimming pool	One must be very careful when diving.

PART I: **Punctuating with Connectives**

Punctuate the following sentences properly. If the sentence requires no punctuation, write a C after it:

1. People who want to be truly successful in life need to have a clear sense of values as well as direction.
2. They need to know what is most important to them and they must pursue the attainment of that goal.
3. Of course there are many individuals who achieve enormous material success without a proper sense of values.
4. Many people have even obtained great wealth because of their lack of values.
5. These people however eventually find that they have nothing except the material goods they have worked so hard to obtain.
6. Even the most beautiful expensive items become meaningless when they become the focus of one's life.
7. On the other hand individuals who place greater emphasis on serving God and helping other people than on achieving their own personal goals may not obtain a great level of material wealth but they enjoy enormous spiritual emotional, and personal satisfaction.
8. This satisfaction is critical to a truly successful life.

PART II: **Cause and Effect**

Write a one-page cause and effect essay. In the first paragraph, give the cause. In the remaining two or three paragraphs, explain the effects. This essay may be based on a real incident or it may be purely fictional. If you are completing this course in a group with several other students, all of the participants should share their essays and make comments.

PART III: Comparison and Contrast

Write a two-page essay of comparison and contrast. The first page should provide the comparisons; the second page should provide the contrasts. You might choose your subject from the following list:

Compare two people you know well

Compare two organizations (for example, Boy Scouts and Girl Scouts)

Compare two foods (chocolate ice cream and spumoni)

Compare two kinds of music (classical and jazz)

Choose subjects with which you have enough familiarity and personal experience to create an effective comparison/contrast.

PART IV: Expository Writing

Write a one-page expository essay. Take the reader step-by-step through a process or an event with which you are familiar. Really think about this assignment before you begin writing, or you will tend to leave out important steps/events. Possible topics for this exercise include:

How to Grow (Tomatoes, Bell Peppers, etc.) Choose one item only!

How to Bake a Cake

How to Change a Tire

Once again, choose a subject with which you are familiar. Read this essay and the others in this unit exam to your friends or family members, and ask for their input.

I'll call for pen and ink, and write my mind.

SHAKESPEARE, *I HENRY VI* (1591)

UNIT FIVE

Writing that Convinces the Reader

LESSON TWENTY-TWO: PERSUASIVE WRITING

These are the times that try men's souls. The summer soldier and the sunshine patriot will, in this crisis, shrink from the service of their country; but he that stands by it now deserves the love and thanks of man and woman. Tyranny, like hell, is not easily conquered; yet we have this consolation with us, that the harder the conflict, the more glorious the triumph. What we obtain too cheap, we esteem too lightly: it is dearness only that gives everything its value. Heaven knows how to put a proper price upon its goods; and it would be strange indeed if so celestial an article as freedom should not be highly rated. Britain, with an army to enforce her tyranny, has declared that she has a right (not only to tax) but "to bind us in all cases whatsoever" and if being bound in that manner is not slavery, then there is not such a thing as slavery upon earth. Even the expression is impious; for so unlimited a power can only belong to God.

I have as little superstition in me as any man living, but my secret opinion has ever been, and still is, that God Almighty will not give up a people to military destruction, or leave them unsupportedly to perish, who have so earnestly and so repeatedly sought to avoid the calamities of war by every decent method which wisdom could invent. Neither have I so much of the infidel in me, as to suppose that He has relinquished the government of the world and given us up to the care of devils; and, as I do not, I cannot see on what grounds the king of Britain can look up to heaven for help against us...

The heart that feels not now is dead; the blood of his children will curse his cowardice, who shrinks back at a time when a little might have saved the whole and made them happy. I love the man that can smile in trouble, that can gather strength from distress, and grow brave by reflection. Tis the business of little minds to shrink; but he whose heart is firm, and whose conscience approves his conduct, will pursue his principles unto death. My own line of reasoning is to myself as straight and clear as a ray of light. Not all the treasures of the world, so far as I believe, could have induced me to support an offensive war, for I think it murder; but if a thief breaks into my house, burns and destroys my property, and kills or threatens to kill me, or those that are in it and to "bind me in all cases whatsoever" to his absolute will, am I to suffer it? What signifies it to me, whether he who does it is a king or a common man; my countryman or not my countryman; whether it be done by an individual villain, or an army of them? If we reason to the root of things, we shall find no difference; neither can any just cause be assigned why we should punish in the one case and pardon in the other.

Thomas Paine, *The Crisis, Number 1*

By the time you have completed this lesson, you should be able to do the following:

- Understand the principles of persuasive writing.
- Identify the basic techniques used to persuade readers.

Persuasive writing is designed to convince the reader to think, feel, and act in a certain way. Persuasiveness is an art used in many aspects of our everyday lives. Children attempt to persuade their parents not to punish them for misbehaving. Teenagers use persuasion when trying to convince their fathers to let them borrow the car. Friends use persuasion when trying to get each other to go on blind dates. Politicians use persuasion to try to get people to vote for them. Marketing agencies use persuasion when trying to get people to buy their products.

In the example on the preceding pages, Thomas Paine uses persuasive techniques to make his point that refusing to fight against Great Britain during the American Revolution is not noble, but is, in fact, cowardice. What arguments does he use to support this proposition?

Following are some of the techniques of persuasion used by advertisers. They are also used by salespeople and many speakers. Study these, and then look at the advertising in your own home to see how many of these techniques are being used:

Bandwagon

Everybody is doing it, and so should you. This is a favorite tactic for children who want to convince their parents to let them do something, but it is also frequently used by adults. Commercials touting statistics about how this or that is the bestselling car, or perfume, or stereo in the nation, use the bandwagon technique.

Plain Folks

The people who use this product or this service or believe this idea are people just like you. This is a favorite for politicians who generally try to portray themselves as "common men" so that the common man can identify with them.

Testimonial

This product or service is used by a famous television star, sports star, or other type of celebrity. If you like the person, you should use the same product. There are numerous examples of this technique in all advertising. All celebrity endorsements are testimonials, but celebrities also campaign for politicians and for certain causes. They use their reputations and fame to persuade other people to join the cause.

The Desire to be Set Apart

This technique is used to advertise very expensive or exclusive products. It carries the idea that only "special" or "important" people use a certain product, drive a certain car, stay in certain hotels, etc. If you use this product, you, too, will be special. For examples of this kind of advertising look at advertisements for all luxury automobiles.

Card Stacking

The advertiser or salesperson tells only a partial truth and leaves out all of the information which would make his product or idea look less desirable. There is an element of card stacking in nearly all advertising. For example, if an advertisement states that a dealership wants to sell a $20,000 car for $200.00 a month, it is certain that some very important information about the payment terms is being omitted.

Glittering Generalities

The idea or product is "new," "redesigned," "best," or "wonderful." Glittering generalities capture the interest of the other person without giving any real information about the product, service, or idea. Look at the products on the aisles of the supermarket to see how many have the words "New" or "Improved" on their packaging. The idea is that people will purchase a new product simply because it is new.

Of course, persuasion should never be used to deceive or take advantage, but all persuasion is based on appealing to the needs and desires of the audience.

What elements are essential to persuasive writing? First, appeal to the desires of the audience. People are motivated by certain basic desires such as the desire for ease and comfort, for the privileges of the wealthy, for beauty, for youth, and for luxury. Appealing to these desires makes it possible to persuade people to buy a certain product or to use a certain service. Convince the reader that his best interests are most important and that the idea, product or service will make his life easier. Study the following example of persuasive writing. To what desires does this ad appeal?

> Every conscientious homeowner should have a Black & Decker leaf blower. Few things are more tedious than bending over a conventional rake in an attempt to clear your yard of thousands of unsightly leaves. Using conventional methods, you expend hours of back-breaking work to clean your yard. With a Black & Decker leaf blower, however, work time is cut in half. Just flick a switch, and in no time leaves are effortlessly blown from your yard. So why risk destroying precious grass using a harmful rake? The Black & Decker leaf blower will blow your yard free of debris and leave the grass for your enjoyment.

PRACTICE

Exercise A:

Imagine that you are selling a product. You may choose any product you wish. Write an advertisement for the product. Convince your audience that your product is superior to everyone else's and that they should buy your merchandise rather than that of someone else.

Exercise B:

Imagine that you are running for political office. Sell yourself to the public in a short campaign speech. Tell the public what you have to offer and what you will do for the voters. Convince them that you are a better candidate than your opponent.

GRAMMAR CHECK

Subject/Verb Agreement: Clauses

When relative clauses are used, the subject and the verb in the clause must agree. If the *antecedent*—or word to which the pronoun refers—is singular, the relative pronoun is also singular. If the antecedent is plural, the relative pronoun is plural. A plural verb must be used with a plural pronoun and a singular verb with a singular pronoun.

Study the following examples carefully. The italicized word in each sentence is the relative pronoun. The other words in boldface make up the relative clause:

Example:

Rebecca is one of the students *who* **win every year.**

(In this sentence, the word *win* refers to *students,* which is plural. Rebecca is part of a group of students who win every year.)

Rebecca is the only one of the students *who* **has received a medal in penmanship**.

(In this sentence, only Rebecca received the medal. Therefore, the word *who* refers to the antecedent *one.)*

In deciding whether to use singular or plural verbs in relative clauses, look to see whether the clause refers to a group of people or to just one person in the group. If the clause refers to the actions of the entire group, use the plural verb. If it refers to the actions of only one member of the group, use the singular verb.

Self-Check Test

Choose the correct verb for each sentence:

1. Gena Riley is one of the people who (have/has) perfect attendance.
2. Winesaps are one of the many varieties that (is/are) classified as apples.
3. This table is the only one of the group that (have/has) survived one hundred years.
4. The tutti-frutti shake is one of the many flavors that (is/are) available.
5. Raspberry is the only one of the flavors of ice cream that (has/have) been discontinued.
6. Walking is the only one of the many aerobic activities that (is/are) safe for almost everyone.
7. Jogging is one of many exercises that (is/are) popular.
8. Pizza is one of the foods that (is/are) best liked in the United States.
9. Hamburgers are the only one of the fast foods that (is/are) cheap.
10. Mark Twain was one of the nineteenth century writers who (has left/have left) an impression on society.

GRAMMAR CHECK

Subject/Verb Agreement: Prepositional Phrases

Do not confuse a word which is part of a prepositional phrase with the subject. The simple subject is never part of the prepositional phrase. Find the subject and make the verb agree in number with the subject. Cross out the prepositional phrases that may come between the subject and verb if that helps.

Study the following sentences. The simple subject and the verb appear in bold type. The prepositional phrase is italicized.

The **owner** *of the ships* **is** Mr. Davidson.

The **house** *on the hill* **is** mine.

The little **puppies** *under the table* **belong** to me.

The shy **girls** *across the room* **are** my sisters.

Notice that the prepositional phrase does not change the verb.

Self-Check Test

Underline the prepositional phrase in each of the following sentences. Then, underline the subject twice. Finally, choose the correct form of the verb needed to complete the sentence:

1. The people near the river (is/are) our neighbors.
2. The girls beside the house (is/are) sisters.
3. The frogs of Green Lake (come/comes) out every spring.
4. The bird above the trees (is/are) an eagle.
5. The canary with the golden feathers (sing/sings) beautifully.
6. The friends across the room (belong/belongs) to the same organization.
7. The man inside the barn (has been/have been) working.
8. The grass outside the walls (has/have) grown.

9. The two girls in the office (is/are) good friends.
10. The paintings opposite the mirror (was painted/were painted) by a famous artist.

GRAMMAR CHECK

Shifting from Active to Passive

In the *passive voice,* the subject receives the action. In the *active voice,* the subject does something. Study the following sentences:

Passive:

The bill was explained to me by the mayor. (The bill receives the action.)

Active:

The mayor explained the bill to me. (The mayor performed the action.)

Passive:

I was nominated student body president by the class. (I received the action.)

Active:

The class nominated me student body president. (The class performed the action.)

Passive:

Albert Einstein was considered stupid by his teachers (Einstein received the action.)

Active:

His teachers considered Einstein stupid. (The teachers performed the action.)

Passive:

The building was condemned. (The building received the action.)

Active:

City officials condemned the building. (The city officials performed the action.)

Both the active and passive voices are acceptable, although generally active voice is preferred because it is less awkward. Do not, however, shift from active to passive voice in a sentence when the same person or thing is still performing the action. Such a shift results in writing that is *non-parallel* and difficult to read:

Non-Parallel:

He studied the law, set up a practice, and a fortune was made.

Parallel:

He studied the law, set up a practice, and made a fortune.

Self-Check Test

The following sentences combine active and passive voices. Rewrite each sentence in the active voice:

1. Jamie went to Milwaukee, found a job, and a new life was started.
2. June won the election and was given the oath of office.
3. The fishermen caught the fish, cleaned them, and a great catch was taken to the market.
4. The trees grew big, spread out their leaves, and a lovely shade was created for the animals.
5. The prisoner pled guilty, was sentenced by the judge, and his execution took place shortly.
6. The citizens' group fought city hall, voiced their disapproval of the bill, and the legislation was defeated.
7. Mary Lee worked in the restaurant, struggled to keep her family alive, and her dream of having a better life was realized.
8. The chickens lived in the yard, laid eggs for the family, and at Christmas a chicken dinner was served.
9. The committee drafted the proposal, drew up their recommendations, and the complete document was submitted to the chairman.
10. Janie ran for office, managed her own campaign and was elected by the people.

PUNCTUATION CHECK

Knowing When to Underline

Underline words and phrases that are being defined or discussed specifically:

The word communicate comes from a Latin word meaning "to make common."

Good little children say please and thank you.

Underline words that come from non-English languages and are still considered foreign:

Adios is Spanish for good-bye.

The attorney asked for a writ of <u>habeas corpus.</u>

Underline the titles of books and magazines:

<u>Ladies Home Journal</u> is a popular women's magazine.

I have just finished reading <u>Les Miserables</u>.

Use quotation marks to set off the names of chapters in a book, articles in a magazine, short stories or poems:

Mrs. Johnson read "Ten Cooking Tips" in this month's <u>Ladies Home Journal.</u>

"Children of Adam" was not included in Walt Whitman's <u>Leaves of Grass.</u>

Note: the rules about underlining apply to handwritten essays. When using a word processor, *italicize* all phrases that would be <u>underlined</u> in a handwritten essay.

Self-Check Test

Underline or use quotation marks where necessary in the following sentences:

1. The Knitting Done is a chapter in A Tale of Two Cities.
2. Mrs. Morris was reading How to Be a Good Mother in Redbook.
3. Little House on the Prairie and Little House in the Big Woods are books by Laura Ingalls.
4. Daucus pusillus is more commonly known as rattlesnake weed.
5. Where I Lived and What I Lived For is a chapter from Henry David Thoreau's Walden.
6. Haute couture is the industry of leading women's fashion houses.
7. The hors d' oeuvres included stuffed mushrooms and shrimp cocktail.
8. To corrupt is to change from a sound to a putrid state.
9. National Geographic contains many interesting articles.

10. Webster's Dictionary is a useful resource book.

GRAMMAR CHECK

Subject/Verb Agreement: Inverted Sentences

Inverted sentences are ones in which the subject appears after the verb. As with sentences in natural order, the subject and verb must agree.

Remember that when the words *there* or *here* begin a sentence, these words are never the subject of the sentence. Look for the subject after the verb. Study the following examples:

There is the man. (*Man* is the subject; *is* is the verb.)

Here are the flowers. (*Flowers* is the subject; *are* is the verb.)

There are the cats. (*Cats* is the subject; *are* is the verb.)

Here is the spoon. (*Spoon* is the subject; *is* is the verb.)

In questions, an auxiliary (helping) verb may begin the sentence. The subject often comes between the auxiliary verb and the main verb. In the following examples, the auxiliary and main verbs are italicized while the subject of each sentence appears in bold:

Does **the woman** *work* here?

Do **the children** *play* in the valley?

Self-Check Test

Choose the correct verb for each sentence:

1. There (is/are) two basic reasons for buying a durable car.
2. Here (come/comes) the salesman.

3. (Do/Does) you visit your grandmother often?
4. (Has/Have) Mr. Jenkins heard the news?
5. (Here (lie/lies) the bones of the great Civil War hero.
6. There (go/goes) the mayor of the city.
7. (Was/Were) Laura coming to the party?
8. (Am/Are) I going with you?
9. Here (is/are) the site of the great battle.
10. There (was/were) no clear victor.

GRAMMAR CHECK

Subject/Verb Agreement: Linking Verbs

A linking verb which connects the subject with a predicate nominative must agree with the subject, not the predicate nominative. Study the following examples:

The trees *were* the only vegetation.

Mr. and Mrs. Hanson *were* the only life in sight.

The letters *stand* as a testimony of her intent.

The people *were* a mass of opposition.

The dogs *serve* as ornaments.

Remember: Always find the subject of the sentence first. Make the verb agree with the subject—not with any other word in the sentence.

Self-Check Test

Choose the correct forms of the verbs below:

1. Television news shows (have become/has become) a primary way of making money for the networks.
2. Reporters seen every night on television (have taken on/has taken on) celebrity status.
3. These men and women (become/becomes) symbols of information and integrity to many Americans.
4. Interviews with famous people (are/is) a major draw for audiences.
5. Further, the television news show (represents/represent) an inexpensive vehicle which makes a great deal of money.
6. It is no wonder that the success of the older news shows (has resulted/have resulted) in a huge block of imitators.
7. Stars such as Diane Sawyer (is/are) models for many aspiring reporters.
8. Now that a number of shows (have become/has become) successful, there will be many others.
9. We can expect that the high ratings (is/are) a major incentive in the production of such television shows.
10. Television news shows (is/are) likely to be a lasting trend.

UNIT TEST

PART I: Subject/Verb Agreement

Read the following sentences. If the subject and verb agree, write a C after the sentences. If they do not agree, rewrite the sentences correctly:

1. These are the best friend I ever had.
2. Here is the dishes you need for the party.
3. There is the kittens.
4. These is the things you asked me to bring.
5. Here come the boys and Jane.
6. The legislation require that all paperwork be in on time.

PART II: Prepositional Phrases

Underline the prepositional phrases in each sentence below:

1. Down the hall and under the table ran the little cat.
2. People who live in glass houses should not throw stones.
3. Over the river and through the woods to grandmother's house we go.
4. For the reasons I have just cited, this will be critical to your career.
5. I will meet you at the café in the morning.

PART III: Underlining

Underline all the words and phrases which should be underlined in the sentences below. Put quotation marks around those words and phrases which require them:

1. Good Housekeeping contains the interesting column Good Cooking.
2. I wanted to get some tips on growing Mr. Lincoln roses, so I bought the May issue of Better Homes and Gardens magazine.
3. The Secret Sharer is a riveting story by Joseph Conrad.

4. Anne of Green Gables and Anne of the Island are books by Canadian author Lucy Maude Montgomery.
5. When I was in school, I read Jane Eyre by Charlotte Bronte and Ben Hur by Lew Wallace.
6. Junta is the Spanish word for council.

PART IV: Persuasive Writing

Imagine that you are currently receiving an allowance of $7.00 a week from your parents. You want a cost of living increase to $8.50 a week. Write a persuasive paragraph arguing in favor of the raise. Clearly state why you believe that you deserve to receive an additional $1.50 a week. Be prepared to answer your parents' objection that they cannot afford to give you a raise. In your essay, state what you can offer to them in exchange for the additional money.

This essay should be approximately one page in length. When you are finished, read it to your family or friends and get their feedback. Then revise your essay to make your arguments stronger.

What is written without effort is in general read without pleasure.

SAMUEL JOHNSON, *MISCELLANIES* (C. 1776)

UNIT SIX

Writing for Work and for Pleasure

LESSON TWENTY-THREE: WRITING WITH QUOTATIONS

"What's the matter?" I asked in my ordinary tone, speaking down to the face upturned exactly under mine.

"Cramp," it answered, no louder. Then slightly anxious, "I say, no need to call anyone."

"I was not going to," I said.

"Are you alone on deck?"

"Yes."

I had somehow the impression that he was on the point of letting go the ladder to swim away beyond my ken—mysterious as he came. But, for the moment, this being appearing as if he had risen from the bottom of the sea (it was certainly the nearest land to the ship) wanted only to know the time. I told him. And he, down there, tentatively:

"I suppose your captain's turned in?"

"I am sure he isn't," I said.

He seemed to struggle with himself, for I heard something like the low, bitter murmur of doubt. "What's the good?" His next words came out with a hesitating effort.

"Look here, my man. Could you call him out quietly?"

I thought the time had come to declare myself.

"I am the captain."

I heard a "By Jove!" whispered at the level of the water. The phosphorescence flashed in the swirl of the water all about his limbs, his other hand seized the ladder.

"My name's Leggatt."

The voice was calm and resolute. A good voice. The self-possession of that man had somehow induced a corresponding state in myself. It was very quietly that I remarked:

"You must be a good swimmer."

"Yes. I've been in the water practically since nine o'clock. The question for me now is whether I am to let go this ladder and go on swimming till I sink from exhaustion, or—to come on board here."

Joseph Conrad, The Secret Sharer

By the time you have completed this lesson, you should be able to do the following:

- Understand the proper use of quotations.
- Incorporate quoted material into your writing.

To *quote* someone is to relate the individual's exact words—copying exactly what the speaker said so that the message, in context, is repeated for the reader. Certain rules of punctuation apply to quoted material. These rules are particularly important when writing dialogue between two characters so that the reader will know exactly who is talking at all times.

When quoting someone's exact words, use quotation marks. Quotation marks are placed directly before and after the words spoken so that the reader can easily determine which ideas were stated by the speaker and which statements were made or implied by the writer.

Example:

"Where are you going?" asked John.

In the above example, the quotation marks are placed around the exact words spoken by John in order to separate those words from the remainder of the sentence. It would be **incorrect** to punctuate the sentence as follows:

"Where are you going, asked John?"

In the above example, John did not say, "asked John," as part of his statement. Quotation marks are used only around the speaker's words.

The first word of a quotation is capitalized. A comma separates the quoted material from the *credit tag*—the phrase identifying the speaker. Study the following examples:

"Please come open the window," *said Shirley*.

Shirley said, "Please come open the window."

"Please," *said Shirley*, "come open the window."

The credit tag may appear at the end of the quoted material, at the beginning, or in the middle. Regardless of its location, it is always separated from the quoted material by some final form of end punctuation—such as a question mark or an exclamation point—or by a comma. Do not use a comma when a question mark or an exclamation point has been used.

Punctuation is included inside the quotes if it is relevant to the quoted material. For example, the question mark is included in the quotes if the quoted statement is a question. However, if it is not the quoted material, but rather the statement as a whole that is a question, the question mark appears outside the quotation marks:

Linda asked, "Will dinner be ready before 5:00?"

Do you think it was she who said, "I will be here on time"?

Study the following examples of quoted material carefully:

"Have another cup of coffee," the hostess offered.

The pilot announced, "Fasten your seatbelts."

"Is that real gold?" asked the old prospector.

The horrified neighbor screamed, "The house is on fire!"

"Look, it's the Easter Bunny!" squealed the delighted child.

"If you want something done right," grumbled the angry man, "you've got to do it yourself."

"Do you want to go with me to the store?" asked Mother. "I'm leaving right now."

Notice that in each example, a comma or some other form of end punctuation separates the credit tag from the quoted material. When the quotation is divided so that the credit tag appears between two parts of the quoted statement, do not use a capital letter at the beginning of the second phrase unless it also is a complete sentence. Notice the last two sentences above.

The same principles which are used in writing a one-sentence quotation apply to a conversation. The most important rule to remember when writing a conversation is that each new speaker begins a new paragraph. When two individuals are having a conversation, start a new paragraph each time the speakers change. Study the following conversation noticing the punctuation:

"What are you still doing with that lion?" Cindy asked. "I thought that you took him to the zoo."

"I did take him to the zoo," Tom replied.

"Then what is he doing here?"

"Well, we had so much fun that now we're going to the movies!"

Notice that when Cindy finished speaking and Tom began, we started a new paragraph. Likewise, when the conversation switched from Tom back to Cindy, another new paragraph was begun. This is necessary to make it clear to the reader who is speaking. Notice also that no credit tag was used for the last two sentences. Yet, it is very clear that Cindy made the first statement, and Tom made the last one. It is not necessary to use a credit tag in a very long dialogue if it is clear to the reader which character is speaking each phrase. If there is any room for doubt, however, leave the credit tag. Use the tag when more than two speakers are talking.

He Said/She Said

"Says" and "states" should not always be used to introduce quoted material. Below is a list of alternative words which can open and close quotations. Study this list carefully; not all the words on this list have exactly the same meaning so it would be wise to check them in a dictionary before actually applying them to a conversation:

acknowledged	assured	confessed	dictated
acquiesced	directed	attested	confided
added	avowed	contended	disclosed
admitted	begged	contested	divulged
addressed	boasted	continued	elaborated
advised	bragged	contradicted	enjoined
advocated	called	counseled	entreated
affirmed	charged	countered	enunciated
agreed	equivocated	chided	debated
alleged	exclaimed	claimed	decided
announced	commanded	declared	explained
argued	complained	demanded	granted
articulated	conceded	denied	held
asked	concluded	denounced	hesitated
assented	concurred	described	hinted
imparted	observed	reasoned	responded
implored	ordered	rebutted	revealed

indicated	petitioned	recited	ruled
inferred	pleaded	recognized	stated
informed	pointed out	stipulated	recounted
inquired	prayed	refuted	suggested
insisted	preached	regretted	supplicated
insinuated	proclaimed	reiterated	supposed
interrogated	pronounced	rejoined	swore
interjected	proposed	related	talked
intimated	protested	remarked	testified
lamented	proved	reminded	thought
lectured	queried	remonstrated	told
lied	questioned	repeated	translated
maintained	quibbled	reported	urged
mentioned	quipped	replied	uttered
narrated	quoted	reprimanded	vowed
noted	ranted	requested	warned
objected	read		

Self-Check Test

Exercise A:

Punctuate the following sentences correctly using quotation marks, capital letters, commas, periods, exclamation points, and question marks:

1. hang your coat in the hall closet said marsha
2. careful the floor is wet and slippery warned the janitor
3. mother snapped do not run in the house.
4. last night I shot a bear in my pajamas quipped groucho marx how he got in my pajamas I shall never know
5. the little boy asked is there any such thing as santa claus
6. the frightened child cried where is my mommy
7. you have to calm down explained the police officer because I cannot understand you
8. you have been working for hours you must be tired why don't you stop and rest suggested mark
9. I think the dog ran away I haven't seen him anywhere announced dad
10. Joey keeps hitting me and I didn't do anything to him sobbed the little boy
11. take this money exclaimed uncle joe and hide it where the police won't find it
12. do you ever wonder if there are aliens on other planets questioned the student
13. stand there ordered mary and don't move until I tell you
14. the waiter asked are you ready to order
15. the circus trainer shouted step right up and see the man-eating tiger
16. if you are not ready to leave by now called her impatient boyfriend you never will be

Exercise B:

The following conversation has been written without any paragraphing, punctuation, or capital letters. Rewrite it correctly:

where have you been complained jason the weather is getting really bad dont you think I know that retorted mike i was the one getting rained on out there anyway I was looking for my dog spot I cant find him anywhere I think the thunder scared him off do you think we should go out again and look for him asked jason he could be killed in a storm like this sure lets go said mike not so fast you two called mother from the other

room the dog will find his own way home you two sit down
and eat your soup

Exercise C:

Write a one-page dialog between two characters. Use the alternative words from the list in this lesson to begin each line of quoted material. Begin your dialog with this sentence, "As Jill was briskly walking her dog on a September morning, she unexpectedly bumped into Jack."

GRAMMAR CHECK

Avoiding Double Negatives

Double negatives occur when *no* is used twice in the same expression. Double negatives are always grammatically incorrect. Study the following sentences. The first sentence contains a double negative. In the second sentence one of the negatives has been removed to make the sentence correct:

Incorrect:

> Johnny didn't have no time to eat.

Correct:

> Johnny didn't have time to eat.

Or:

> Johnny had no time to eat.

In the first sentence, the word *didn't* tells us that Johnny could not eat. By adding the word *no* we have created a double negative. Either the second or third sentence is a correct alternative to this.

Some common expressions such as *could hardly* and *could scarcely* are negative. Do not add the words *no* or *not* to these expressions.

Incorrect:

We couldn't barely start the car.

Correct:

We could barely start the car.

Incorrect:

We couldn't scarcely finish the cake.

Correct:

We could scarcely finish the cake.

Note: the word *regardless* is already negative. Never say *irregardless*.

Self-Check Test

Correct the following sentences containing double negatives by rewriting the sentence to contain only one negative:

1. Diana could not hardly finish her meal.
2. She would have gone with him, but she did not have nobody to take care of the baby.
3. Eric could not scarcely get his horse up the hill.
4. James did not have no idea what was happening.
5. Mark could not get no more help from his parents after he told them a lie.
6. The dog would not drink no more water.
7. You should not buy no more flour until we use what we have.
8. David would not play with the older children no more after the fight.
9. The cat does not come around no more since I yelled at her.

10. I will not try no more to get you to change your mind.

Be particularly careful in everyday writing to avoid negative words and expressions. Review each paragraph to make certain that no double negatives occur. Review this section often to refresh your memory about the use of negatives.

PUNCTUATION CHECK

Using Commas for Special Information

Use commas between units of measurement:

> The athlete was *six feet, five inches tall.*

> The new baby weights *eight pounds, six ounces.*

Use a comma to separate the chapter number in a book from the page number:

> I found the information I need in *Chapter 7, page 413.*

Use a comma to set off a light interrupter in sentences. When addressing someone directly, use a comma after the person's name:

> *Mark,* go to the store.

> Here is the information you requested, *Mr. Smith.*

> Thank you for your help, *Mrs. Martin.*

Use a comma to show what someone thought or that something is true:

> The papers, *Henry thought to himself,* are missing.

> The cost of the scanner, *Sally believed,* was too expensive.

Use a comma to start a sentence with *yes, no, well,* or *why:*

>*No,* I do not want to play tennis.

>*Well,* what did you really expect?

Use a comma to add a short question that is addressed to your listener:

>You are going with us, *aren't you?*

>The coat is rather expensive, *don't you think?*

Use a comma to add something for contrast after *not* or *never:*

>Janet, *not Bill*, prepared the essay.

>They met at her house, *never in the garden.*

Self-Check Test

Exercise A:

Insert commas where needed in the following sentences:

1. Yes I plan to read Chapter 6 page 24 of the novel.
2. Mary please get me the butter and sugar.
3. John is six feet three inches tall and weighs two hundred twenty pounds fourteen ounces.
4. I really appreciate everything you have done for me Mr. Stevens.
5. You read the book didn't you?
6. Margaret not Johnny is the head of the committee.
7. Jeannie plays with her doll never with the truck.
8. Why I had no idea that Missy and George were engaged.
9. Well if you really wanted my help you should have asked for it Mark.
10. This place Joan thought to herself will never be suitable.

Exercise B:

Write ten original sentences following the pattern of the above ten. Be certain to insert commas where they belong.

PUNCTUATION CHECK

Commas in Dates and Addresses

Use a comma between the day of the month and the year in the date:

> *July 4, 1776*　　　　　*June 17, 1982*　　　　　*March 14, 1914*

When the date is followed by other information in the sentence, use a comma after the year also. If only the month and year are given, however, the comma is not necessary:

> The war lasted from *September 2, 1939,* to *August 8, 1945.*

> The business operated from *May 17, 1978,* to *June 5, 1985.*

> World War II ended in *August 1945.*

Use a comma between the day of the week and the date:

> The celebration began *Monday, April 5,* and ended *Saturday, April 9.*

Use a comma between the parts of an address. The comma should appear between the name of the street and the name of the city and between the city and the state:

> I live at *1515 Westmoreland, Boston, Massachusetts.*

> The neighbors moved to *1232 Green Street, Stockton, California.*

Self-Check Test

Insert commas where they belong in the following sentences:

1. On June 1 2011 I moved to my new home at 10500 Oak Avenue New York New York.
2. The wedding will take place Saturday November 9 2012.
3. Mrs. Myrtle wrote to me from her hotel at 25 South Street London England.
4. July 14 1789 is a very important date in French history.
5. October 12 1978 was the birth of their first child.
6. From Tuesday September 10 through Sunday September 14 the Greens will be having their open house.
7. The historic celebration took place Tuesday June 9 1952 through Thursday June 11.
8. You may write to us at 1595 Brook Street Philadelphia Pennsylvania 10725.
9. On Monday October 6 the neighbors arrived.
10. Friday January 6 will be my last day with this company.

PUNCTUATION CHECK

Numbers and Abbreviations

Abbreviate only the words that are commonly accepted as abbreviations. Such words include titles such as:

Mr., Mrs., Dr., St., Jr., and Sr.

Degrees are also abbreviated:

M.D., LED, PhD

Abbreviate A.D. and B.C. and A.M. and P.M. (**Note**: do not use A.M. with the phrase "in the morning." Likewise do not give the time as 10:00 P.M. "in the evening." The initials A.M. or P.M. indicate the time of day.)

Use the initials of the names of agencies, business forms and other organizations that are commonly known by their initials:

Johnny worked for the FBI before going to work for IBM.

Use the initials of geographical locations which are commonly known by their initials:

Washington D.C. is the capital of the United States.

My brother spent a year in the U.S.S.R. before communism collapsed there.

Abbreviate the units of measurement which are commonly known by their abbreviations such as mph and rpm. Do not abbreviate the other units of measurement.

Use numerals when a decimal point is required. Use numerals for exact sums of technical measurements. Numerals should also be used for addresses, dates, years, street numbers, and page numbers:

I was born June 5, 1968, at 1026 Maple Avenue.

I have read up to page 218 of the novel.

Spell out the numbers from one to ten, numbers requiring no more than two words and any number at the beginning of a sentence. Compound numbers from 21-99 must be hyphenated:

The new baby weighed six pounds, four ounces.

Twenty-one people survived the crash.

One hundred individuals are currently enrolled.

Self-Check Test

The following sentences contain no abbreviations. Abbreviate only those words that should be abbreviated. Also, write in numerals those numbers that should be numerals:

1. The porcelain doll cost one hundred twenty-five dollars and sixty-five cents.
2. Jeanne went to work for American Telephone and Telegraph after she finished school.
3. John's mother moved to one hundred five North Avenue, Washington, District of Columbia.
4. Six entries were chosen as the prize winners in the one hundred thousand dollar drawing.
5. I rise as six o' clock ante meridiem.
6. My parents did not arrive back in town until eleven o' clock post meridiem.
7. Mister Jones and Doctor Johnson had an interesting conversation about Saint Patrick.
8. The letter was signed, "Harry Burton, Doctor of Philosophy."
9. Mark Harris, Junior will meet Mark Harris, Senior for lunch on Friday.
10. In the year twelve hundred fifteen Anno Domini, King John signed the Magna Carta.

LESSON TWENTY-FOUR: WRITING BUSINESS LETTERS

By the time you have completed this lesson, you should be able to do the following:

- Understand the components of a business letter.
- Compose well-organized business letters of your own.

Business letters are written to a business associate, a company, or a professional person. They are generally written when making a complaint to a company, when ordering a product or a service through the mail, when communicating with associates, when applying for jobs, and for other professional reasons.

Study the following example of a business letter written as part of a job application:

44 South Street
Dallas, Texas 75512
March 6, 2011

HEADING

Mr. Mark Jones
HR Director
United Bank of Texas
121 Westway
Dallas, Texas 75249

INSIDE ADDRESS

209

Dear Mr. Jones: **SALUTATION**

                                   BODY

I am writing in response to the job posting on Jobsareus.com, for a supervisor for the residential mortgage lending department of the Dallas/Fort Worth branch of the United Bank of Texas. Enclosed is my resume detailing my education and my work experience.

I recently moved to Dallas from Colorado where I worked at Colorado State Bank supervising the mortgage department for two and one half years. Prior to becoming a supervisor, I was a residential loan originator for five years for a small mortgage company in Denver. During my years in Colorado, I worked with numerous underwriters and personally closed over $10,000,000 in business per year for three consecutive years.

I am very interested in this position, and I believe that my past work history has given me the experience that will give me an edge in your company. I am available for an interview at your convenience. You may contact me at the address or telephone number on my resume.

Thank you for your time and consideration.

Sincerely,   **COMPLIMENTARY CLOSE**

Paul Stevens   **SIGNATURE**

In the sample letter above, the *heading* is placed in the upper right corner. The next part of the business letter is the *inside address* which is placed two lines beneath the heading. The inside address appears on the left side of the page. The inside address is, of course, the address of the business. Make a point of finding out the name of the person who will receive the letter and the correct spelling of his name; be sure to include it at the top of the inside address. Also be sure to include his title. Following the name and title of the recipient are the business name, address, city, state, and zip code.

Two lines beneath the business address is the *salutation*. In a business letter, the generally accepted salutation is *Dear Sir or Madam* when the name of the person to whom the letter is going is unknown. There is an excellent possibility that a woman will answer the letter, and if it has been addressed to *Dear Sir* or *Gentlemen,* she may be offended. Of course, in cases where the recipient of the letter is known, it is important to address the letter directly to that person. Use *Ms.* when writing to a woman in business. (In most business correspondence, and particularly in a cover letter for a job application, it is very important to address the letter to a specific individual.)

The salutation in a business letter is always followed by a colon. DO NOT use a comma after the salutation in a business letter. Commas are too informal for the formal style required in a business letter.

Next is the *body* of the letter. The sample letter above is a letter of application for employment. The text of the letter will be determined by the author's reason for writing it. It is very important, however, that the letter be clear, concise, and easy to understand. Generally, the letter should be long enough only to communicate the required information.

At the end of the letter, place the *complimentary close* followed by the *signature*. The best and most widely accepted complimentary close is *sincerely,* although *respectfully* is also often used. The complimentary close is followed by a comma.

Business letters should always be typed. The letter should be single-spaced with an inch margin on each side; it should begin ten spaces from the top of the page and should be centered on the page. After the complimentary close, the writer spaces down four single spaces and types his name. Between the complimentary close and the typed signature, he signs the letter.

A business letter should be well-written and to the point. Its purpose should be clearly stated so that the person receiving the letter knows exactly why it was written and what it is intended to accomplish. It should clearly state what action, if any, ought to be taken as a result of the letter.

Study the following example of a letter of complaint. Notice that the writer states clearly in the opening paragraph why she is writing:

1000 Anywhere Street
Average Town, New Mexico 55555
September 6, 2011

Mr. Mike Feeley
Rental Manager
Paul Todd Realty
5555 Willow Lake
Average Town, New Mexico 55555

Dear Mr. Feeley:

I am writing to complain about your handyman, Frank. I have called him on four separate occasions to repair my dishwasher, and he never returns my calls. My dishwasher has not worked for over a month.

Last week you sent him to my house to fix the handle on the front door. Frank looked at the handle and said he would have to buy a part from the hardware store. He promised to return in approximately twenty minutes. Although the hardware store is only about five miles away, Frank did not return with the part until the following day.

You need to be aware of the problems with Frank's reliability. He should be notified that he is greatly inconveniencing your tenants.

Please let Frank know that it is imperative that he become more reliable. His undependable work habits are causing a hardship on my family and me.

Sincerely,

Sue Smith

In the following letter to the editor of a local newspaper, the writer is communicating an opinion and does not require a response. Nevertheless, the writer clearly identifies the issue to which he is responding and what his opinion is on that issue:

1000 Anywhere Street
Average Town, New Mexico 55555
December 4, 2010

Mr. James King
Issues Editor
Average Gazette
5600 Park Street
Average Town, New Mexico 84567

Dear Mr. King:

I am writing in response to the article, "Is Congressman Flakey Measuring Up?" which appeared in the Sunday, June 2, 2011, edition of the "Issues" section of The Average Gazette. The article was an interview with Congressman Donald Flakey discussing the tax cuts that Flakey has promised to support if he is re-elected to his seat in Washington.

I, personally, am disgusted by politicians who promise much and do little. Congressman Flakey has held his seat in Washington for twelve years, and during all that time he has voted against every tax cut that has ever been presented to him.

If Flakey were genuinely concerned about the burdens of the taxpayers, he could surely have found some solutions during his first twelve years in office. Promises from Washington mean nothing to small business owners and families struggling in a tough economy.

Congressman Flakey and his Washington cronies need to wake up and understand that we here in Average Town are tired of empty promises. We need a Congressman who will take action. I am afraid that Congressman Flakey is not the man for the job.

Sincerely,

John Williams

PRACTICE

Write a letter for each of the following situations. After you have completed your letters, let your study partner look at them and tell you whether you have stated your points clearly.

Exercise A:

You have seen Carter's ad for a floor manager in the children's clothing department. Tell the company why you are writing, where and when you saw the advertisement, and what the ad said. State your qualifications for this position. Try to convince the company that you are the best qualified applicant for the job. Apply to:

Carter's Department Store
1221 Matthew Avenue
St. Louis, Missouri 52510

Exercise B:

Your local newspaper has run an editorial entitled, "Separation of Christmas and State, Please," expressing the view that nativities are unconstitutional and should not be on city property. Many people in the community support continuing a public nativity. Write a letter to the editor clearly stating your position on the

214

subject of whether your city should allow nativity displays on public property. Address your letter to:

Ms. Marilyn Flighty
Editor
Average Gazette
5600 Park Street
Average Town, New Mexico 84567

GRAMMAR CHECK

Using Commas in a Series

When listing a series of items, use a comma after each item to set it apart from the others. Study the examples:

cats, dogs, horses, carriages

apples, oranges, pears, nectarines

The comma may be omitted before the word *and*. However, the comma before *and* is always correct, and it should be used in formal writing.

Use a comma to set apart phrases describing a series of actions or naming a series of items:

Jane's favorite activities are *reading books, watching television,* and *talking on the telephone.*

I like *cherry pie, vanilla ice cream,* and *hot coffee* on rainy days.

She wore *a purple sweater, purple scarf, black skirt,* and *purple blouse* to church.

Use commas between adjectives or adverbs in a series. Do not use a comma after the last adjective or adverb in the series:

Big, black, hairy bears live in the zoo.

Slowly, quietly, and *cautiously* the man approached the large dog.

Self-Check Test

Exercise A:

In the following sentences insert commas where they belong:

1. Marissa likes to ski hike and play tennis.
2. Lisa's favorite foods are lasagna spaghetti and spumoni ice cream.
3. Lion's tigers and bears live in the woods.
4. Glass steel and brick are common building materials.
5. Farmers engineers and miners all work outdoors at times.
6. Girl Scouts Boy Scouts and Little League are organizations that serve children.
7. Martha and Jane got up early went to the store bought groceries and returned home.
8. Martin gathered the information wrote up his findings typed the report and submitted it.
9. Great round marble arches graced the entrance to the ancient majestic city.
10. Slowly precisely and meticulously the carpenter cut the fine-grained oak slabs for the cabinets.

Exercise B:

Now write ten original sentences containing series of your own. Be sure to use a comma after each item in your series.

GRAMMAR CHECK

Subject/Verb Agreement: Collective Nouns

Collective nouns are nouns which name groups. A collective noun is singular when it refers to the group as a whole. It is plural when it refers to the individuals in the group:

> The *team wins* every year. (Talking about the group)

> The *team is changing* their uniforms. (Talking about the individual members)

> The *faculty is* the finest in the state. (Talking about the faculty as a group)

> The *faculty are* very unhappy. (Talking about the individual members)

Special Nouns

Nouns such as *mathematics, mumps,* and *measles* take singular verbs:

> *Mathematics is* the hardest subject in school.

> *Mumps is* a child's disease.

> *Measles is* very unpleasant.

Nouns That Name Amounts

When the noun names *an amount that is one unit*, it is singular. When the noun refers to *the individual amounts*, it is plural:

Singular:

> *One hundred dollars is* the cost of the jacket.

Plural:

> *One hundred dollars are* in the bank.

Singular:

> *Six months feels* like an eternity to a child.

Plural:

> *Six months are spent* studying each year.

Titles

A title is always singular, no matter how many words it includes:

> *Anne of Green Gables* is my favorite book.

> *Jane Eyre,* by Charlotte Bronte, is a book about a young woman in England.

The Number v. A Number

The number is singular. *A number* is plural.

> *A number* of the teammates *are winning.*

> *The number* of dropouts *is growing.*

Compound Subjects Joined By Or or Nor

When a compound subject is joined by *or* or *nor,* it requires a singular verb. The subjects are being considered separately:

> Fred *or* Jim is coming to your party.

Neither Harry *nor* Tom was present.

Compound Subjects with Many A, Every, and Each

When the words *many a, every,* and *each* precede the subject, the subject is usually singular:

> *Many a* student learns the hard way that studying matters.

> *Every* good boy does fine.

> *Each* little bird has a beautiful song.

Self-Check Test

Choose the correct verb for every sentence below:

1. The jury (delivers/deliver) its verdict.
2. The jury (were/was) three housewives, a teacher, and a minister.
3. Ten thousand dollars (is/are) the price of the boat.
4. Twenty dollars (is/are) on the table.
5. Mathematics (is/are) the only subject I really disliked in school.
6. Measles (is/are) a dangerous disease.
7. *A Tale of Two Cities* (is/are) a book by Charles Dickens.
8. Michael or Johnny (is/are) needed in the office.
9. Neither the dog nor the cat (like/likes) the cold weather.
10. Many a great individual (have/has) ruined his life with bad decisions.
11. A number of students (was/were) waiting in the halls.
12. The number of children who attended (is/are) amazing.
13. Every person here (has/have) helped.
14. Each of the birds (is/are) more beautiful than the next.
15. Seven years (is/are) a very long time to wait for what we want.

LESSON TWENTY-FIVE: WRITING IN THE DIGITAL AGE

By the time you have completed this lesson, you should be able to do the following:

- Understand writing in the context of the digital age.
- Understand how to apply your skills to blogs, emails, and social networking sites.

The last decade has revolutionized communications in the United States through the wide spread usage of email, blogging, and social media sites. Ten years ago, Facebook did not exist—today the site has more members than the population of the United States. Five years ago Twitter was just beginning—today its membership stands at more than half of the population of the U.S. The use of social networking and digital platforms are changing the way we write, relate to others, and communicate in the 21st century.

The internet, in general, and the use of social networking sites and blogs, in particular, provide the aspiring writer with amazing new avenues for publication. A writer who, in the past, would have had to spend a lot of time sending out query letters for an opportunity to see even one article published can now set up a blog and publish his opinions to the whole world. This new world creates a lot of new opportunity and new responsibility for writers. A magazine article from twenty years ago could be buried in an old issue never to be seen again. In the digital age, however, a blog or article that appears on the internet stays there indefinitely to be viewed by readers worldwide.

In this section, we will explore some of the most common forms of writing in the digital age so that you can produce work that you can be proud of today and ten years from now.

Email

Email is one of the most common forms of online communication, and it is the one that you will probably encounter most frequently in a professional setting. While more formal communications still require business letters prepared on letterhead, most informal business communication is done through email. In an era where we do business transactions not only in our own cities and states, but across the country and around the world, email correspondences are sometimes the only impression that a potential customer or colleague will have of us. For that reason our email communications are critical.

When writing an email, start with the subject line. The subject line is important because it separates your email from SPAM emails. Be clear and to the point. If the email is about a real estate closing on Saturday, an appropriate subject line might be, Re*: Closing on 1152 Main Street Road, Saturday*. This alerts the recipient that your email has specific information that he needs to open and read.

Here are some basic tips for writing office emails:

Be polite: Acknowledge the recipient's name. If you are sending an email in response to a telephone conversation, acknowledge that you have just spoken with the person. Don't be too chatty, but take a moment to recognize that you are talking with a human being.

Be professional: Write your email in complete sentences. Check the spelling of all words, including the subject line. Capitalize and punctuate properly. Your email correspondence says a lot about your level of professionalism—if you don't take your emails seriously enough to proofread them, probably nobody else will take you very seriously either.

All professional emails should include an address tag. This can be directly programmed into most email applications. You should include your name, title, company, address, phone number, fax number, and email address. That way, if the recipient of your email needs to pick up the phone to speak with you, he won't have to hunt around for your phone number—he will have it as part of your communication. No matter how many times you correspond by email with a person, have your address tag on the bottom of each one.

Be concise: Email allows you to communicate very quickly and to respond quickly to questions. Many professionals are receiving hundreds of emails each day, and they don't want to devote a lot of time to reading any one individually. State clearly what you want to say, and keep it brief.

Be careful: Because of the nature of emails, they can travel quickly from person to person. Many careers have been ruined because the sender made comments that he later wished he could retract. Remember, once you hit the "send" button there is no going back. As a general rule, do not say anything in an email about a person that you would not say to that person directly. If you are angry or distressed about a situation, you probably should not send an email until you have had a chance to think carefully about what you need to say. Words typed in anger will reverberate for a long time, can permanently damage your relationships, and can even cost you your job. People tend to be braver in emails than they would be in face to face confrontations, but the consequences of this bravado can be far-reaching.

Be respectful: Even if you are not upset when you are writing an email, you may appear angry or authoritarian if you do not word your email properly. Read it before sending to make sure that it conveys the tone you want. Don't type your email subject lines or any part of your email in ALL CAPS—it may appear to the reader that you are shouting at him.

Below is a sample of an email for a real estate closing:

> Subject: Re: Closing for 12345 Weatherford Lane, Any Town, New Mexico
>
> Hi, Anna:
>
> As we discussed on the telephone I have emailed you the updated contract that I need to have Jake and Molly Smith sign to close on their new home. I have spoken with Bill at

Any Town Bank, and I understand that he has already sent you all of the mortgage documents for the closing. Please confirm that you have received everything you need. Please also let me know the exact amount that Jake and Molly need for their cashier's check prior to 5:00 P.M. Friday.

The closing is scheduled for 10:00 A.M. this Saturday at your office. The seller will be closing at 9:30. Jake and Molly will be moving in this weekend. We will need to make sure that they have a complete set of house keys and the garage door openers for the new property.

It has been a pleasure to work with you on this file. I look forward to seeing you Saturday morning as we close and give Jake and Molly the keys to their new home.

Sue Cramer
Sunshine Realty
1145 Any Street
Any Town, New Mexico 88888
(575) 555-5155 Phone
(575) 555-5255 Fax
sue@sunshine.net

When replying to a business email, the same rules of professionalism, respect and courtesy apply.

Hi, Sue:

Thanks for the follow up. I appreciate your sending the copy of the contract. Bill did send me the closing documents, but I am still in need of the closing instructions. He says that I will have them in an hour. I can get you the dollar amount that Jake and Molly need by early tomorrow morning. If you have a survey, please send it to me.

As always, Sue, it has been great working with you and your buyers. I look forward to seeing all of you on Saturday morning.

Anna Gomez
Any Town Title Company
1305 Any Street
Any Town New Mexico 88110
(575) 555-4444 Phone
(575) 555-2222 Fax
anna@anytowntitle.com

Many of the people you correspond with through business emails may request a "read receipt" from you. The reason for this request is to verify that you have seen the information. You should always respond by sending a "read receipt" so that the person with whom you are communicating knows that you received the information. You should also program your toolbar to request a "read receipt" for your professional emails. This will save you many follow up phone calls.

Blogs

Blogging is a great tool for creative expression and inexpensive small business marketing. Many sites, such as Blogger, offer users an opportunity to set up free blogs. Blogs can be personal in nature, but they can also be used for expression of political or religious ideas.

In business, blogging can be an excellent addition to a small business marketing plan. Blogging regularly can keep your website information fresh. It can also help raise other companies' awareness of your business.

I read recently about a woman who ran a very small cabinet company. She wrote a regular blog which had a handful of readers. One day in her blog she mentioned a difficulty that she was experiencing with a major company with which she was attempting to do business. The president of that company performed automatic searches of all blogs and internet postings referring to his company, and he saw her blog. He got in touch with her, corrected the problem, and opened the door for her very small company to begin to do business with his large company.

As with other information on the internet, the contents of blogs stay in cyberspace indefinitely. Because of this, the content that is posted is very important.

The same rules apply to blogging that apply to email and other forms of communication. Be polite, be respectful, be professional and be careful. While a well-timed, well-thought-out posting may open doors for you professionally, a careless one can cost you jobs or relationships in the future. Since that is the case, think carefully about what you are writing before you write it.

As with all other forms of writing, each blog post should have a topic and all of the information in the blog should support the topic. Information that does not support the topic should be deleted.

The following excerpt is from a blog on parenting and homeschooling:

> Christmas weekend we took our grandchildren to see the new *Narnia* movie, *The Voyage of the Dawn Treader*. In this story Lucy is fixated on being as beautiful and popular as her older sister Susan, and in one scene stands in front of a full-length mirror comparing her appearance to Susan's. As she stares at her image, she sees herself morph into Susan. She then steps into the mirror and finds herself at an outing where she is the center of attention. As she basks in her new-found popularity, however, she discovers that when she became Susan, Lucy had ceased to exist, either in the past or the present. As a result, all of Lucy's contributions to the family had disappeared along with her, and Narnia had never been discovered. Lucy is then pulled back through the mirror and Aslan appears beside her. When she asks what happened, he replies, "You wished yourself away."
>
> I believe that this may be the most important lesson in this latest theatrical release in the Narnia series. It is a lesson that is especially appropriate for this time of year when many of us are preparing our New Year's resolutions—most of which will be some version of losing weight and/or going to the gym regularly. As a society we long to be someone "better" than who we are. We are constantly exposed to people who are better looking, smarter, better educated, and more successful than we. As a result, we try to remake ourselves into their images. We begin to believe that if we were better looking, smarter, better educated, or more successful that other people would value us and we would lead more fulfilling lives. We end up wanting to be almost anyone other than who we are.
>
> It is, of course, important to always look for ways to improve ourselves, but it is equally important to recognize that we already have value. God loves diversity and He made each of us unique.

While it is true that you cannot become someone else, it is equally true that someone else cannot become you. You have special work to be done in a special way that is unique to you. If you were suddenly to morph into that person whom you admire so much, who would do those things God entrusted to you? The truth is that God's world would have a little hole in it shaped just like you.

I hope that as you prepare your New Year's resolutions you will give serious thought to the things that need work in your life and make a genuine effort to improve in those areas. I also hope that you will remember that you are God's unique creation. He made you exactly the way He wanted you to be, and no one else can take your place. Whatever else you do in the New Year, don't wish yourself away.

In this blog post, the author makes the point that we should appreciate ourselves as God made us. Each sentence in the post supports this topic.

Facebook, Twitter, and Other Forms of Social Media

Facebook, Twitter and other forms of social media are increasingly popular avenues for communication. These social networking sites allow users to post comments, website links, and video links to share with friends in the network. As social networking sites grow in popularity, the types of sites will grow also. For now, the two most popular sites are Facebook and Twitter.

Facebook started as a social networking site for college-age adults, but over the past couple of years it has grown into a huge marketing engine for businesses. Many businesses and organizations maintain a Facebook page for their companies, and some companies maintain multiple pages. With over 500 million users, Facebook has become a major force in our modern world and a huge avenue for exposure.

Facebook fan pages include product pages, pages for reality television shows or news organizations that allow viewers to interact with celebrities on line, pages for authors and publishers that allow authors to host product giveaways, and pages for radio stations that allow fans to communicate with and interact with radio program hosts. As the presence of Facebook grows, the opportunities for interactions will as well. Comments made to one group of Facebook friends can be "shared" by friends or fans with their own groups of friends or fans with the result that information can spread rapidly across the site.

Twitter is a very different type of site from Facebook. Twitter is just a little over five years old, so it is a younger site than Facebook. Users send "tweets" limited to 140 characters. Any message which is over 140 characters must be condensed or shared in the form of multiple tweets. Twitter offers followers the ability to forward tweeted messages by "retweeting" to members of their own group. Because of this ability to retweet, messages can be spread rapidly throughout the Twitter network and shared with a potential audience of more than 190 million people.

The importance of paying careful attention to what we post on line cannot be overstated. More and more employers are routinely checking social networking sites as part of the employment-screening process. They are looking for compromising photos or evidence of behavior which would reflect badly on their organization. Employers can also continue to check social networking sites after the hire to make sure that the information posted does not embarrass the organization.

Information posted on the internet is basically impossible to remove, and it can impact your life for many years. Think carefully before you write or post anything. If you are wondering whether something is appropriate to post, ask yourself this question, "If everyone in the world saw this post/photo/video, etc. would I be embarrassed?" If the answer to that question is "yes" don't post it because if you do you are giving everyone in the world an opportunity to see the material.

PRACTICE

These exercises test your writing skills with emails and blogs. If you are under eighteen, you must ask permission of your parents before doing anything on the internet. If the internet is unavailable to you, you can still complete the exercises by following the guidelines below, but rather than posting them you will be simply completing the exercises as a written paper:

Exercise A:

Larger cities feature "Food Paparazzi"—bloggers who visit restaurants and write about specific dishes. These amateur food critics write blogs that give travelers and tourists a lay person's perspective on where to find the best food in a new city. This exercise allows you to join their ranks.

Write a blog post comparing your favorite dish as prepared by different restaurants. For example, if macaroni and cheese is your favorite dish, compare the macaroni and cheese at three dining establishments. For instance, perhaps one restaurant serves macaroni and cheese with bacon while another serves it with bread crumbs, and a third serves it plain. Your posts should state clearly which dishes you preferred and why, and what you found lacking in some of the other dishes and why.

Food paparazzi photograph the dish to go with the blog. If you have access to a camera phone or a digital camera, you can discreetly photograph your dish for your post before eating it. Be discreet and respect the feelings of the wait staff and chef.

(As an alternative to comparing professionally-prepared meals, you can do this at home by comparing three homemade dishes. For instance, you could compare hot dogs grilled by your dad to hot dogs grilled by your neighbor and your uncle.)

The point of the exercise is to be creative. Write your post in such a way that your audience really understands why you prefer one dish over another. If you are able to post this as a blog along with a photo of each dish, invite your friends and family to read what you have written and comment in the comments' section.

Exercise B:

You have just gotten a new job as the executive assistant for the director of a local chamber of commerce. As her assistant, you are responsible for keeping up with all of her appointments. Your first day, you discover that she has appointments scheduled to attend three events at one time. The first event is a major fundraising meeting with Fred Smith, a key donor to the organization. The second event is a ribbon-cutting for a new member. The third meeting is an appointment with the mayor and representatives of city council on a zoning ordinance which the organization opposes.

Your boss must attend the meeting with the donor as scheduled. She needs to reschedule the meeting with the mayor and city council for later in the afternoon. She cannot attend the ribbon cutting at all, but as her executive assistant you will be attending in her place.

Write an email to each of these entities introducing yourself and explaining the schedule. To the donor, Fred Smith, you will send an email confirming the appointment and thanking him for taking time to meet with her. To the mayor and members of city council, you will ask to reschedule the meeting until later in the afternoon. To the new member, you will thank her for her membership and explain that you will be attending the ribbon cutting for her new business on behalf of the organization.

After you have finished this exercise, have several people read your emails and make comments. If you have a friend or family member who will pose as the recipient of the email, you can trade emails on each of these topics. Remember that this is an exercise in professionalism, so write something that will make your new boss proud!

LESSON TWENTY-SIX: WRITING PERSONAL ESSAYS

By the time you have completed this lesson, you should be able to do the following:

- Understand and define personal essays.
- Compose a personal essay of your own.

When we know the basics of paragraph writing, we can easily extend our skills to essay writing. Essays are simply compilations of related paragraphs which tell a story or relate information to the reader.

The length of the essay depends upon the subject matter and the purpose for which it is being written. Personal essays are usually not very long—generally 5-7 paragraphs totaling about 500-700 words. In academic writing, the length of the essay will almost always be determined by the instructor's guidelines, and these guidelines should be followed as closely as possible.

All essays follow basically the same format. The first paragraph provides an introduction. This is followed by several paragraphs which make up the body of the essay and provide supporting evidence for the topic stated in the introduction. Finally, the writer concludes with a closing paragraph which summarizes the main point of the essay.

The introduction and the conclusion are very important. Abraham Lincoln once said that to create an excellent speech the speaker needs a fabulous opening and a slam-bang finish, and then he should put them as close together as possible. In a way, this is also true in writing. The opening needs to be interesting enough to capture the reader's attention. The opening must also be specific and to the point so that the reader will be able to immediately identify what the subject matter of the essay is and what specific aspect of that subject matter will be discussed in the essay. The introduction must contain a *thesis statement*. The thesis statement is a sentence or a group of sentences stating the main idea or central message of the essay. When the reader asks himself the question, *"What is the subject of this essay?"* he should find the answer to that question in one or two sentences in the first paragraph. Those sentences are the thesis statement.

The conclusion is also important. Because it is the final impression that is left with the reader, much consideration should be given to it. Conclusions, as well as introductions, are more difficult to write than the body of the essay because they require more creativity and originality. Consequently, many people end their essays too abruptly by skimping at the end. Do not do this! A conclusion can make or break the essay. If the conclusion is effective, the reader will come away with a clear understanding of the issues. If, on the other hand, the conclusion is weak or sketchy, the reader will come away confused or unimpressed.

A conclusion is the best place for reinforcement of ideas. Generally, it is a summary of topics, ideas, or events discussed in the body of the essay. It is also the acceptable place for the writer to express his opinions. In personal essays it is generally acceptable for the author to express his opinions throughout the essay; in other formal types of essays, the writer is required to remain more objective.

Be careful not to be too repetitive in the conclusion. In summarizing, review previously mentioned ideas, but do not restate everything that has already been discussed in the body of the essay. Do not quote sentences from another part of the essay in the conclusion. Good conclusions are often brief and to the point.

The body of the essay is rather simple. It consists of several paragraphs providing information and discussing the subject of the essay. Each paragraph has its own topic sentence and supporting sentences providing evidence for the topic. Every sentence in each paragraph must relate directly to the topic sentence. When changing topics, subjects, or ideas, begin a new paragraph. Likewise, each paragraph must relate directly to the thesis statement. No matter how interesting an idea or a subject is, if it does not relate directly to the thesis sentence, leave it out.

PRACTICE

You are now ready to begin writing personal essays. Because such essays are based on personal experience and perspective, they require no research. They are, therefore, easy beginning essays.

Write a personal essay on *one* of the following topics. Be sure to include an introductory paragraph in which you state your thesis sentence, two or three paragraphs for your body, and a final concluding paragraph in which you summarize your main points:

Topics

1. Write an essay describing your first three months in high school or college. Explain the problems you encountered and the adjustments you had to make to become comfortable with your new routine.
2. Describe a special talent you have such as playing the piano, painting, cooking, etc. Discuss the way in which you developed the talent and the way you use it for your own enjoyment and that of others.

WORD CHECK

Using Good and Well, Bad and Badly

To answer the question, "*How was it done?*" use the adverbs *well* and *badly*. To answer the question, "*What was it like?*" use the adjectives *good* and *bad*. Remember that adjectives modify nouns while adverbs modify verbs, adjectives or other adverbs. The following sentences illustrate the proper use of *good* and *well:*

The hot cocoa was very *good*. (What was it like?)

She prepared it very *well*. (How was it done?)

A *Tale of Two Cities* is a *good* book, and my little boy reads it *well*.

Her manners were *good*; she behaved *well*.

This is *good* work; you have completed the assignment *well*.

It is incorrect to say that a person "looks good." When you ask someone, "*How does he look?*", the correct response is to say that the person "looks well." It is also incorrect to say that someone "feels good." Instead, say that he "feels well." This is also true of *bad* and *badly*. Never say that a person "feels badly." This indicates that he is unable to feel the object he touches. Instead, say that he "feels bad." This means that he feels ill or unhappy. Study the following examples of the correct uses of *good, well, bad,* and *badly*:

After the *bad* accident, he was *badly* injured.

Since her *bad* fall, she plays tennis *badly*.

She looked *well* after her week at the spa.

He felt *well* after exercising for twenty minutes.

He felt *bad* about having been rude to his wife.

Self-Check Test

Choose the correct word for each sentence:

1. The pain was (bad/badly).
2. Her leg hurt (bad/badly).
3. He acted (bad/badly), and now he feels (bad/badly).
4. The trip went extremely (good/well).
5. The station (bad/badly) needs organization.
6. Mrs. Johnson looks (good/well) since her surgery.
7. The (bad/badly) management has caused a series of mistakes.
8. The food was (good/well). I prepared it (good/well).
9. The food was (bad/badly). The chef prepared it (bad/badly).
10. The company is (good/well) controlled by the (good/well) management.
11. Juan felt (bad/badly). He had been treated (bad/badly).
12. Their sick child is getting (good/well).
13. I feel (good/well).
14. I feel (bad/badly).

GRAMMAR CHECK

Using Sit/Set and Lie/Lay

To *sit* is to be seated. To *set* is to put an object at rest. Study the following chart to see the correct forms of *sit* and *set*. **Remember:** Today I *sit* in this chair; yesterday I *sat* in this chair; I *have sat* in this chair; I *am sitting* in this chair. Likewise, today I *set* the object on the table; yesterday I *set* the object on the table; I *have set* the object on the table; I *am setting* the object on the table. Review the chart below to increase your understanding of these verbs.

Present tense	Past tense	Perfect tense	-ing form
sit	sat	sat	sitting
set	set	set	setting

Study the following sentences in which *sit* and *set* are used correctly:

> In the summer I *sit* in the sun all day.
>
> *Set* the vase of flowers on the table.
>
> She *sat* down in the chair.
>
> They *set* their luggage in the front hall.

Likewise, *to lie* is to be at rest. *To lay* is to put at rest. *Remember:* Today I *lie* down to rest; yesterday I *lay* down to rest; I *have lain* down to rest; I *am lying* down to rest. Today I *lay* the books on the desk; yesterday I *laid* the books on the desk; I *have laid* the books on the desk; I *am laying* the books on the desk. The chart below will help to reinforce the proper usage of these verbs:

Present tense	Past tense	Perfect tense	-ing form
lie	lay	lain	lying
lay	laid	laid	laying

Study the following examples demonstrating the correct use of the forms of *lie*:

In the summer I *lie* in the sun all day.

On Saturday mornings, I *lie* in bed.

I *lay* in bed until 10:00 yesterday morning.

I *lay* in the sun for three hours last week.

I *have lain* in the sun for hours.

The body *had lain* there for days.

I must stop *lying* in the sun so much.

Remember that in the present tense *lay* always means to set something at rest. Study the following sentences which demonstrate the correct use of the forms of *lay*.

I will *lay* my purse on the table for now.

I am going to *lay* the records on top of the stereo.

I *laid* my credit cards near my purse.

We *have laid* the tile in the bathroom.

We *have laid* the reports on his desk.

He is *laying* the papers on the desk right now.

Self-Check Test

Choose the correct form of *lie, lay, sit,* or *set* for each sentence below:

1. After (laying/lying) my papers on the table, I went out to (lay/lie) in the sun.
2. (Sit/Set) down the vase, and (sit/set) down and talk with me.
3. He had (laid/lain) the last of the tile before he had (laid/lain) down to sleep.
4. I (laid/lay) down my purse before I (laid/lay) down to sleep.
5. During the winter we let the dog (lie/lay) on the kitchen floor.
6. Matilda is (sitting/setting) the dishes on the table.
7. (Lay/Lie) the coats in the bedroom.
8. (Sit/Set) still for a few moments.
9. She had (laid/lain) down her purse before she entered the room.
10. The book is so good it is impossible to (lay/lie) it down.
11. (Sit/Set) the flowers by the bookcase.
12. Father always (lay/laid) down for a nap after dinner.
13. He had (laid/lain) down to sleep earlier that morning.
14. They have (laid/lain) their luggage by the door.
15. Maria (sat/set) down in the chair when she arrived.
16. She is (sitting/setting) still now.
17. I am going to (lie/lay) down now.
18. He (lay/laid) the books on the table.
19. They are (lying/laying) the tickets on the counter.
20. If you let the dog (lie/lay) on the floor, he will refuse to leave the house.

Practice making the *lie/lay, sit/set* distinction in all of your writing. Whenever you use these words, double-check to make sure that you have used the correct forms. Review this section often to refresh your memory.

WORD CHECK

Other Commonly Misused Words

Principal/Principle

A popular mnemonic for remembering that the principal is the head of the school is the saying, "The principal is your pal." It is important to know, however, that *principal* refers to the main or primary official while *principle* refers to a conviction or an idea.

Following are some other commonly misused words:

Discrete/Discreet

Discrete means separate or distinct; *discreet* means modest or having good judgment:

> The *discreet* spy remained *discrete* from the other members of the group.

Compliment/Complement

Compliment can be a verb meaning to praise another person, or it can be a noun for the affirmation itself. *Complement* means to complete (in fact, it is related to the word *complete*):

> The hostess received many *compliments* on her chocolate cheesecake; it was the perfect *complement* to the meal.

Noisome

This is an uncommon word, but when it is used, it is often used improperly. *Noisome* has its origins in French and is related to the word *annoying*. It actually refers to something that is annoying or offensive to the senses, particularly to the sense of smell. Often the word *noisome* is confused with the word *noisy:*

> The food was a *noisome* concoction of fat and salt.

Realtor

The word *Realtor* is always capitalized because it designates someone who is part of the association of Realtors. If you are not certain whether an individual should properly be referred to as a *Realtor,* use *real estate agent* instead.

Appraise/Apprise

To *appraise* is to assess or evaluate, and it is used primarily in reference to placing a value on property. To *apprise* is to give information:

> After *appraising* the two-acre property, the Realtor *apprised* the seller that the land was not worth the asking price.

Enormity/Enormous

Enormity[9] refers to something which is extremely immoral. *Enormous* refers to something which is extremely large:

> Even the most jaded people in the community were shocked by the *enormity* of the crime.

> Mr. and Mrs. Jenkins built an *enormous* house in the middle of town—when they died, their children donated it to the museum.

Healthy/Healthful

These two words are so often misused that the misusage is becoming correct. The old rule is a good one to know, however. *Healthful* indicates that a certain thing is good for you; *healthy* means in a state of good health. Food can be healthful; lifestyles can be healthful; people and animals are healthy:

---

[9] According to *Merriam Webster's Dictionary of the English Language*, the use of *enormity* to designate size has become standard. If you use the word in this sense, however, you will come under heavy criticism from usage experts.

After marrying Mandy, Peter adopted a more *healthful* lifestyle, and as a result he became very *healthy*.

Mantle/Mantel

A *mantle* is a cloak; a *mantel* is found above the fireplace:

The weary traveler removed his *mantle* and set his hat on the *mantel*.

Horde/Hoard

A *horde* (noun) is a crowd of people. To *hoard* (verb) is to store up:

He *hoarded* his gold because he feared that marauding *hordes* would take everything away and leave him penniless.

Self-Check Test

Circle the correct word in parentheses:

1. Grape and apple juice are both very (healthy/healthful) drinks.
2. Elijah passed his (mantle/mantel) on to Elisha, his assistant.
3. A (horde/hoard) of people descended on the steps of the capitol to protest events taking place there.
4. Jane and Diane have become very (healthy/healthful) since adopting their new lifestyles.
5. The salad was a perfect (compliment/complement) to the steak.
6. Dick (complimented/complemented) his mother on her good cooking.
7. The combination of grease and heat was very (noisome/noisy).
8. The (enormity/enormousness) of the crime horrified the populace.
9. My little brother brought home an (enormity/enormous) stuffed teddy bear.
10. Last week my father decided that he wanted a wooden (mantle/mantel) for our fireplace.
11. My uncle is a miser; he (hordes/hoards) everything.

12. I was eager to tell everything I knew about the situation, but my friend advised me to be (discrete/discreet).

13. Mother never liked to have a lot of people around her; she always preferred to remain (discrete/discreet).

14. The land in the mountains will probably (appraise/apprise) for a lot of money. I will (appraise/apprise) you of the situation when I have more information.

15. Marti was a (Realtor/real estate agent) because she actually belonged to the Association of Realtors.

GRAMMAR CHECK

Misplaced Modifiers

A *modifier* is a word, phrase, or clause that changes the meaning of a word in the sentence. If a modifier is not placed as close to the word it modifies as possible, the meaning of the sentence will change. One of Groucho Marx's famous lines centers around a misplaced modifier: "Last night I shot a bear in my pajamas. How he got in my pajamas I shall never know." Study the following example of a sentence containing a misplaced modifier:

Mary Ann saw an ancient, gold treasure chest *deep-sea diving*.

Obviously, the ancient gold treasure chest was not deep-sea diving. The sentence needs to be rewritten so that the words *deep-sea diving* are next to *Mary Ann.*

Deep-sea diving, Mary Ann saw an ancient gold treasure chest.

Incorrect:

Our guide told us stories of the shipwrecked sailors he had saved *when he had nothing better to do.*

Correct:

When he had nothing better to do, our guide told us stories of the shipwrecked sailors he had saved.

Self-Check Test

The following sentences contain misplaced modifiers. Rewrite the sentences so that the modifiers are next to the words they modify. Check your answers with the answer key:

1. The taxi driver sped down the street singing loudly.
2. We saw a statue strolling down the street.
3. My purse was found by the banker with my twenty dollars.
4. In the top of the tree I found my Persian cat.
5. I saw a child fall from the top of the building.
6. The child was taken away by his parent who was kicking and screaming.
7. The rose tickled my nose which had long thorns growing from it.
8. My sister married the policeman in an elegant white dress.
9. The candy had been thrown into the wastebasket which was half-eaten.
10. My neighbors ran a very successful store who were Italians.
11. She met her husband for dinner at the bus stop.
12. I walked right into the glass door carrying my yogurt.
13. I went to the movie with my boyfriend which had a scary ending.
14. The dog sat lazily in the grass which had long gray and black hairs on its body.
15. People should not throw stones who live in glass houses.

LESSON TWENTY-SEVEN: AN ARGUMENTATIVE EDGE

They tell us, Sir, that we are weak—unable to cope with so formidable an adversary. But when shall we be stronger? Will it be the next week, or the next year? Will it be when we are totally disarmed, and when a British guard shall be stationed in every house? Shall we gather strength by irresolution and inaction? Shall we acquire the means of effectual resistance by lying supinely on our backs, and hugging the delusive phantom of hope, until our enemies shall have bound us hand and foot? Sir, we are not weak, if we make a proper use of those means which the God of nature hath placed in our power.

Three millions of People, armed in the holy cause of liberty, and in such a country as that which we possess, are invincible by any force which our enemy can send against us. Beside, Sir, we shall not fight our battles alone. There is a just God who presides over the destinies of Nations, and who will raise up friends to fight our battles for us. The battle, Sir, is not to the strong alone; it is to the vigilant, the active, the brave. Besides, Sir, we have no election. If we were base enough to desire it, it is now too late to retire from the contest. There is no retreat but in submission and slavery! Our chains are forged! Their clanking may be heard on the plains of Boston! The war is inevitable; and let it come! I repeat, Sir, let it come!

It is in vain, Sir, to extenuate the matter. Gentlemen may cry, Peace, Peace!—but there is no peace. The war is actually begun! The next gale that sweeps from the North will bring to our ears the clash of resounding arms! Our brethren are already in the field! Why stand we here idle? What is it that Gentlemen wish? What would they have? Is life so dear, or peace so sweet, as to be purchased at the price of chains and slavery? Forbid it, Almighty God! I know not what course others may take; but as for me, give me liberty or give me death!

Patrick Henry, *The War is Inevitable* 1775

By the time you have completed this lesson, you should be able to do the following:

- Define argumentative writing.
- Write an argument of your own.

Mastering the basic concepts of essay writing makes it possible to explore the other kinds of essay writing. Personal essays are interesting because they help the reader learn more about the writer, but they are limited in their subject matter and originality.

Argumentative writing exercises different writing skills. Argumentative writing involves preparing and presenting an argument for or against an issue. The focus of the argument, as well as the approach to the issue, depends largely on the length of your essay and the maturity and intellect of the audience.

One of the greatest examples of argumentative writing is *The Declaration of Independence*. The signers had not only to declare their independence from a foreign power, but they had to persuasively explain their reasons for doing so:

> We hold these truths to be self-evident: that all men are created equal; that they are endowed by their creator with certain inalienable rights; that among these are life, liberty, and the pursuit of happiness. That to secure these rights, governments are instituted among men, deriving their just powers from the consent of the governed; that whenever any form of government becomes destructive of these ends it is the right of the people to alter or abolish it, and to institute a new government, laying its foundation on such principles, and organizing its powers in such form as to them shall seem most likely to effect their safety and happiness. Prudence, indeed, will dictate, that governments long established should not be changed for light and transient causes; and accordingly, all experience hath shown, that mankind are more disposed to suffer, while evils are sufferable, than to right themselves by abolishing the forms of government to which they are accustomed. But when a long train of abuses and usurpations, pursuing invariably the same object, evinces a design to reduce them under absolute despotism, it is their right, it is their duty, to throw off such government, and to provide new guards for their future security. Such has been the patient sufferance of these

colonies; and such is now the necessity which constrains them to alter their former system of government. The history of the present king of Great Britain, is a history of repeated injuries and usurpations, all having in direct object the establishment of an absolute tyranny over these states. To prove this, let facts be submitted to a candid world.

He has refused his assent to laws the most wholesome and necessary for the public good.

He has forbidden his governors to pass laws of immediate and pressing importance, unless suspended in their operation till his assent shall be obtained: and when so suspended he has utterly neglected to attend to them.

He has refused to pass other laws for the accommodation of large districts of people, unless those people would relinquish the right of representation in the legislature—a right inestimate to them and formidable to tyrants only.

He has called together the legislative bodies at places unusual, uncomfortable, and distant from the depository of their public records, for the sole purpose of fatiguing them into compliance with his measures.

He has dissolved representative houses repeatedly, for opposing, with manly firmness, his invasions on the rights of the people.

He has refused, for a long time after such dissolutions, to cause others to be elected; whereby the legislative powers, incapable of annihilation, have returned to the people at large, for their exercise, the state remaining in the meantime exposed to all dangers of invasion from without and convulsions from within.

He has endeavored to prevent the population of these states, for that purpose obstructing the laws for naturalization of foreigners; refusing to pass others to encourage their migration hither, and raising the conditions of new appropriations of lands.

He has obstructed the administration of justice, by refusing his assent to laws for establishing judiciary powers.

He has made judges dependent on his will alone, for the tenure of their offices, and the amount and payment of their salaries.

He has erected a multitude of new offices, and sent hither swarms of officers to harass our people, and eat out their substance.

He has kept among us, in times of peace, standing armies without the consent of our legislature.

He has affected to render the military independent of, and superior to, the civil power.

He has combined with others to subject us to a jurisdiction foreign to our constitution, and unacknowledged by our laws, giving his assent to their acts of pretended legislation.

For quartering large bodies of armed troops among us:

For protecting them, by a mock trial, from punishment for any murders which they shall commit on the inhabitants of these states:

For cutting off our trade with all parts of the world:

For imposing taxes on us without our consent:

For depriving us, in many cases, of the benefits of trial by jury:

For transporting us beyond seas to be tried for pretended offences:

For abolishing the free system of English laws in a neighboring province. Establishing therein an arbitrary government, and enlarging its boundaries, so as to render it at once an example and fit instrument for introducing the same absolute rule into these colonies.

For taking away our charters, abolishing our most valuable laws, and altering, fundamentally, the forms of government:

For suspending our own legislatures, and declaring themselves invested with power to legislate for us in all cases whatsoever.

He has abdicated government here, by declaring us out of his protection and waging war against us.

He has plundered our seas, ravaged our coasts, burnt our towns and destroyed the lives of our people.

He is at this time transporting large armies of foreign mercenaries to complete the works of death, desolation, and tyranny, already begun with circumstances of cruelty and perfidy scarcely unparalleled in the most barbarous ages, and totally unworthy the head of a civilized nation.

He has constrained our fellow-citizens, taken captive on the high seas, to bear arms against their country, to become the executioners of their friends and brethren, or to fall themselves by their hands.

He has excited domestic insurrections among us, and has endeavored to bring on the inhabitants of our frontiers the merciless Indian savages, whose known rule of warfare is an undistinguished destruction of all ages, sexes and conditions.

In every stage of these oppressions, we have petitioned for redress in the most humble terms; our repeated petitions have been answered only by repeated injury. A prince whose character is thus marked by every act which may define a tyrant is unfit to be the ruler of a free people.

Thomas Jefferson, *The Declaration of Independence* 1776

Good, well-written, argumentative writing calls for a certain dedication to your argument. Legend says that when John Hancock signed the Declaration of Independence, he wanted to do so in large enough letters that King George could read the signature without his spectacles. John Hancock believed passionately in his argument, and he was willing to stand by what he wrote with his life if necessary.

When writing an argumentative essay, write about a topic that you have enough interest in to actually defend your position. Topics might range from the importance of protecting rights of gun owners, to ways to help control gang violence in large cities. Think about your audience carefully. To whom is your argument actually directed? You will need to use a different approach when addressing different age groups and maturity levels—the issues which matter to seventh graders obviously differ somewhat from the priorities of senior citizens. Many factors must be considered when preparing an argumentative essay.

Argumentative essays are based primarily on the opinions of the writer. Because they incorporate personal opinions, it is a good idea to choose a topic for the essay which is interesting but not so emotionally charged that it will be impossible to write a sensible argument. Each statement in the argumentative essay should be carefully planned.

After selecting a topic, develop a thesis statement or main idea which will be the central theme for the essay. The main idea will keep the essay focused. Next, establish the supporting points for the essay. Give reasons which will convince the reader that the argument is the correct one. Each of these points should be developed into topic sentences for individual paragraphs. Finally, write a strong conclusion which will not only summarize the major points but will leave the reader convinced of the soundness of the essay's central idea.

PRACTICE

Exercise A:

The first ten amendments to the Constitution of the United States are called the Bill of Rights. The Bill of Rights guarantees 10 basic freedoms to Americans. In fact, in the Bill of Rights are contained many of the most fundamental aspects of law, government and freedom that we celebrate as Americans. However, the application of those rights often leads to arguments as conflicting groups of people claim that they are protected under these rights or that the specific rights in question are being misunderstood or misapplied.

Below are listed the 10 amendments comprising the Bill of Rights. Choose **one** of the ten. Write an essay defending the right in a particular instance. For instance, you might write from the perspective of a gun collector who argues that people should have the right to collect any type of arms under the second amendment. You might write an essay as a pastor defending your town's right to have a public nativity. You might write an essay as a reporter defending your right to free speech.

What is important in this essay is that you focus on ONE right and frame your argument defending that right carefully. You do not have to personally agree with the position you are espousing as long as you write a sound argument:

First Amendment

Congress shall make no law respecting an establishment of religion, or prohibiting the free exercise thereof; or abridging the freedom of speech or of the press, or the right of the people peaceably to assemble, and to petition the Government for a redress of grievances.

Second Amendment

A well regulated Militia, being necessary to the security of a free State, the right of the people to keep and bear Arms, shall not be infringed.

Third Amendment

No Soldier shall, in time of peace, be quartered in any house, without the consent of the Owner, nor in time of war, but in a manner to be prescribed by law.

Fourth Amendment

The right of the people to be secure in their persons, houses, papers, and effects, against unreasonable searches and seizures, shall not be violated, and no Warrants shall issue, but upon probable cause, supported by Oath or affirmation, and particularly describing the place to be searched, and the persons or things to be seized.

Fifth Amendment

No person shall be held to answer for a capital, or otherwise infamous crime, unless on a presentment of indictment of a Grand Jury, except in cases arising in the land or naval forces or in the Militia, when in actual service in time of War or public danger; nor shall any person be subject for the same offence to be twice put in jeopardy of life or limb; nor shall be compelled in any criminal case to be a witness against himself, nor be deprived of life, liberty or property, without due process of law;

nor shall private property be taken for public use, without just compensation.

Sixth Amendment

In all criminal prosecutions, the accused shall enjoy the right to a speedy and public trial, by an impartial jury of the State and district wherein the crime shall have been committed, which district shall have been previously ascertained by law; to be informed of the nature and cause of the accusation; to be confronted with the witnesses against him; to have compulsory process for obtaining witnesses in his favor, and to have the Assistance of Counsel for his defense.

Seventh Amendment

In Suits at common law, where the value in controversy shall exceed twenty dollars, the right of trial by jury shall be preserved, and no fact tried by a jury shall be otherwise re-examined in any Court of the United States, than according to the rules of the common law.

Eighth Amendment

Excessive bail shall not be required, nor excessive fines imposed, nor cruel and unusual punishments inflicted.

Ninth Amendment

The enumeration in the Constitution, of certain rights, shall not be construed to deny or disparage others retained by the people.

Tenth Amendment

The powers not delegated to the United States by the Constitution, nor prohibited by it to the States, are reserved to the States respectively, or to the people.

Exercise B:

A critical component of writing a good argument is understanding the possible objections to your argument. Take the same issue that you wrote about in Exercise A and argue the other side. For example, if you chose gun rights, write an argumentative essay making the case that the Founders did not intend for citizens to keep and bear automatic weapons. If you wrote from the perspective of the pastor, write an opposing argument that public nativities are not protected under the First Amendment. Make a strong opposing argument to whatever argument you made in Exercise A. When you are finished, ask your friends or family members to read both essays and tell you honestly which argument was more compelling.

LESSON TWENTY-EIGHT: PREPARING BOOK REPORTS

By the time you have completed this lesson, you should be able to do the following:

- Understand the major components of a book report.
- Write an effective book report of your own.

Book reports are a frequently assigned part of high school writing. It is important to master the proper technique for an effective book report.

A good book report serves two essential purposes:

- It tells the reader whether a certain book is worth reading.
- It gives someone who has already read the book a chance to gauge his reactions against those of another reader.

An effective review can highlight the major strengths and weaknesses of the book while clarifying areas which the readers may not have understood.

A book report consists of three basic sections. The *synopsis* names the author and the title of the book and summarizes the book's plot. In a review of a fictional work, the synopsis includes the setting, the main characters, and the action of the story. In a review of a nonfiction book, the synopsis outlines the type of information presented and they way in which it is presented.

In the *opinion* section, the writer states how he feels about the book, and in the *support* section he explains the reasons for his opinion. It is important to be extremely specific. Why was a particular book good? For example, "*The Prince and the Pauper* is a really interesting book," is a very vague statement. "*The Prince and the Pauper* is a novel which combines humor and adventure with realistic, likable characters," tells the reader more about why *The Prince and the Pauper* might be worth reading. Other items that belong in a book report include the following:

Setting:

Where does the action of the story take place? In the popular *Anne of Green Gables* novels, Lucy Maude Montgomery chose beautiful Prince Edward Island in Canada as the setting. In this and other similar novels, the setting includes not only the physical location but also the lifestyles and attitudes of the people living there. The setting may be used to shape the characters and their attitudes, or it may stand in sharp contrast to the characters. In *Anne of Green Gables* the very proper home and traditional community in which Anne is raised stand in contrast to her own free-spirited nature.

Characters:

Often, character development is a key element in whether we enjoy a certain book. Why do the characters behave as they do? What experiences or incidents have shaped them into the individuals they are? Are their actions throughout the story consistent with the basic character which has been developed for them? In some stories, the character portrayal is very *flat*; the main characters are either entirely good or entirely evil. In other stories, the characters are more *rounded* and display a mixture of both good and bad traits which make them appear much more human.

Plot:

No review should ever involve a simple retelling of the story, but it should include at least one paragraph discussing the action and events of the story. Discuss how the events of the story shape the characters and reveal their motives. What events move the story forward? Is there conflict in the story, and, if so, how is that conflict expressed? For example, is the conflict between the major characters, or between a character and his environment, or within the character himself as he struggles with his own morals and desires. Some well-placed quotations from the book generally give some additional insight into the plot.

Theme:

When we understand the events which have taken place, we need to then understand their meaning. Why does the author choose these events? What central idea is the author conveying? A complex novel such as Charles Dickens' *A Tale of Two Cities*, which is set against the backdrop of the French Revolution, will not have a simplistic theme such as, "Revolutions are not good." Instead, Dickens uses the revolution to show how individuals who have been treated cruelly react when they have an opportunity for revenge.

Style:

A key part of the way a book affects us is the mood or style. Is the tone serious, humorous, ironic, dark, or lighthearted? How effectively does the author organize sentences, choose his vocabulary, and use the elements of writing to tell his story? A book may be too slickly written, or it may be heavy and clumsily written. The style is generally the primary reflection of the author's writing ability.

The following information may also be included as part of the book report:

The Author:

We generally like to know a little about the author of a book so that we can get some further insight into the book itself. For example, did the author of a book on eighteenth century France actually live in France at that time, or did he live in France at a later time, or has he never been there at all? Was the author of a novel about the sea a sailor himself? The answers to these questions can help us establish the authenticity of a particular work.

The Audience:

Who is the intended audience of a book? A doctor writing an article for a medical journal is writing for other doctors. That same doctor who is writing a diet book for general publication will write very differently because concepts which other doctors will readily understand will be foreign to general audiences.

The Book's Reception:

If a book is a bestseller or a classic, this information may be included in the report. Likewise, if a certain work has received very bad reviews, this might be worth mentioning. On the other hand, some writers prefer to let the reader draw his own conclusions about whether to read the book.

Read the following book report on a nonfiction work:

No Regrets: How Homeschooling Earned me a Master's Degree at Age Sixteen

> *No Regrets: How Homeschooling Earned me a Master's Degree at Age Sixteen* is Alexandra Swann's story of how her mother taught her and her nine brothers and sisters at home from the first grade through master's degrees. Alexandra's story opens one month before her fifth birthday when she begins the first grade, and it concludes when she graduates at age sixteen from California State University with her master's degree in history.
>
> During the intervening eleven years, Alexandra was not only a homeschooled student but also the oldest in a family of ten children. The reader catches unique insights into the Swann family's life from their joyous Christmas celebrations and family gatherings to their struggles through illness and financial difficulties. When Alexandra describes her brother's life-threatening illness, we feel as though we are right there in the hospital with her mother and father. By the end of *No Regrets*, we have gotten to know the Swann family.
>
> "Most parents hope to leave their children something on which to depend when they reach adulthood. My parents have given me the legacy of a good education and a respect for proper values," writes Alexandra at the end of *No Regrets*. This is really the theme of her story. She tells about her childhood in a style that is basically lighthearted and often humorous, but throughout the story she maintains her fundamental theme that education and faith in God are great gifts from a parent to a child.
>
> *No Regrets* has received many positive reviews from leaders in the homeschooling community, including Mary Pride in the *Big Book of Home Learning*. Although this book is about a homeschooling

family, it is not written just for homeschoolers. I enjoyed this book because it is a realistically told story of growing up in a large close-knit Christian family. The Swann family's experiences demonstrate clearly the principle that with faith in God anything is possible. If you enjoy warm, nonfiction books about family life, you will want to read *No Regrets: How Homeschooling Earned me a Master's Degree at Age Sixteen.*

PRACTICE

Read one of the following books and write a book report on it. Be certain to include the synopsis, the opinion, and the support sections as well as comments on the theme and style of the book. When you have completed your review, read it to an audience of family or friends and ask for their comments:

The Prince and the Pauper

Jane Eyre

David Copperfield

The Screwtape Letters

Great Expectations

LESSON TWENTY-NINE: EFFECTIVE TITLES

By the time you have completed this lesson, you should be able to do the following:

- Understand the difference between good and poor titles.
- Create titles that will capture the reader's interest.

When writing a story or essay, make use of good, stirring, effective titles. An interesting title can make an individual curious about the story; the reader may want to read a certain story simply because of the title. On the other hand, a dull, uninteresting title can cause readers to pass the story or essay by.

When choosing a title, be creative. Try to come up with a catch word or phrase which will incorporate the basic spirit and idea of the piece. The title must address the subject matter—it must give the prospective reader a general idea of what the piece is about. How specific the title is usually is determined by the amount of subject matter the written work covers.

For example, the title *Horses* would be acceptable for a book dealing with many different aspects of horses, but it is too broad and vague to be used as a title for a short essay. In a short essay, you would probably be dealing with one aspect of horses such as the ways that man has harnessed their energy throughout the ages. In this case, a title such as *Horse Power* or *The Horse as a Beast of Burden* would be a more specific and appropriate title.

If the work is only a paragraph about horses, the topic should be narrowed further to discuss *one* aspect of *one* particular horse. This might be that horses make pleasurable riding animals, and the essay might focus on the enjoyment of riding a horse. A very specific title is required for this highly focused paragraph. An appropriate title might be *My Horse Lightning is Fun to Ride* or *Riding Lightning.*

Remember that all the important words in the title are capitalized. The only words that are not capitalized are the articles—*a, an,* and *the*—and prepositions. The first word of the title is always capitalized. Do not use any form of punctuation—underlining or quotation marks—around the title at the beginning of an essay or paragraph. It is only when a title is named in a sentence that such special punctuation is needed.

PRACTICE

Each of the following groups describes the type of work which the author is creating—paragraph, short story, book, etc. Each group explains the subject matter of the piece which the author is writing. Listed below this information in each group is a series of possible titles for the work. Based on the subject matter and the length of the work, choose the *most* appropriate title for each:

SUBJECT: *a composition about your love of sky diving*

    a)   Geronimo!!!
    b)   What Color is Your Parachute?
    c)   The Thrill of Sky Diving

SUBJECT: *a cookbook of Greek cuisine*

    a)   It's Greek to Me
    b)   Mastering Greek Cooking
    c)   From Zeus to Prometheus—A History of Greek Cuisine
    d)   Beware of Greeks Bearing Appetizers

SUBJECT: *a paragraph about the best chocolate bar*

    a)   The Best Bar—Bar None
    b)   Hear Say, Hershey
    c)   Sweets for the Sweet
    d)   Willie Wonka and the Chocolate Bar

SUBJECT: *a composition about how to wash a dog*

    a)   Bubble, Bubble, Toil and Trouble
    b)   A Bubble Bath for Benji
    c)   Fuzz in the Tub
    d)   Rub a Dub-Dub

PART I: Business Letters

You are interested in going to work as a salesperson for XYZ Company in Orlando, Florida, selling water softeners. Write a letter of application stating your experience, your education, and your reasons for wanting to work for XYZ. Use the following address:

Mr. Jim Dorndoff
XYZ Company
1315 McGraw
Orlando, Florida 33180

PART II: Essay

Your city has just instituted a 9:00 P.M. curfew for everyone under the age of eighteen. You believe that this curfew is too restrictive. Write a one-page essay arguing against the curfew. Give specific reasons why the curfew should be changed to a later hour.

You are one of the parents who proposed the curfew which is now coming under attack. Write a one-page essay supporting the 9:00 P.M. curfew and giving specific reasons why you believe that it is necessary for the city to maintain it.

PART III: Book Reports

Take one of the books you have read this year and write a book report on it using the basic guidelines you learned in this unit.

APPENDIX

Spelling Guide

In spite of all of the computerized spell checking devices on the market today, many people do not maintain good spelling habits. Even if you rely heavily on your computer to catch your spelling errors, you also need to cultivate good spelling skills. Following are some tried and true spelling rules which will help you become a more accurate speller.

Rule #1

When adding *–ness* to a word that ends in *n*, keep the *n*.

> mean + ness = meanness
>
> thin + ness = thinness

When adding *–ly* to a word that ends in one *l*, keep the *l*. When the words ends in two *l*'s, drop one *l*. When the word ends in a consonant and *–le,* drop the *le:*

> annual + ly = annually
>
> beautiful + ly = beautifully
>
> dull + ly = dully
>
> incredible + ly = incredibly

Rule #2

When adding a suffix that begins with a consonant to a word that ends in an *e,* keep the *e:*

> safe + ly = safely
>
> immediate + ly = immediately

Rule #3

Do not double the final consonant if the accent is not on the last syllable or if the accent shifts when the suffix is added:

> murmur
>
> murmured
>
> prefer
>
> preference

When adding a suffix that begins with a consonant to a word that ends with a consonant, do not double the consonant:

> allot
>
> allotment
>
> regret
>
> regretful

Rule #4

Form the plural of most nouns by adding *s*. If the noun ends in *ch, s, sh, x* or *z*, add *es*.

> cats
>
> dogs
>
> axes
>
> Smiths

Rule #5

Form the plural of most nouns ending in a consonant plus *y* by changing the *y* to *i* and adding *es*.

tries

copies

secretaries

Rule #6

Form the plural of common nouns ending in a vowel and *y* and all proper nouns ending in *y* by adding *s*:

valleys

turkeys

Rule #7

Form the plural of common nouns ending in a vowel plus *o* and all proper nouns ending in *o* by adding *s*:

zoos

patios

Renaldos

Rule #8

Form the plural of common nouns ending in a consonant and *o* by adding *es*. If the noun is of Italian origin and refers to music, just add *s*.

echoes

heroes

cellos

sopranos

Rule #9

Form the plural of most nouns ending in *f* and all nouns ending in *ff* by adding *s*. For some nouns ending in *f*, and those ending in *lf*, change the *f* to *v* and add *es*.

> beliefs
>
> roofs
>
> muffs
>
> leaves
>
> wolves

Rule #10

Form the plural of some nouns ending in *fe* by changing the *f* to *v* and adding *s:*

> knives
>
> lives
>
> wives

Rule #11

Form the plural of hyphenated or multiple word compounds consisting of a noun and modifiers by making the noun plural:

> sixth graders
>
> sisters-in-law
>
> runners up

Rule #12

Certain nouns, particularly those which end in *s*, have the same form in the singular and plural:

series

sheep

deer

corps

Rule #13

Many nouns have irregular plurals:

man	men
woman	women
tooth	teeth
goose	geese
child	children

Rule #14

Certain nouns originating from Latin have different plurals:

crises

data (datum is singular)

media (medium is singular)

beau (beaus or beaux are plural)

Rule #15

Write *i* before *e* except after *c* when sounded like *a* as in *neighbor* or *weigh*:

belief	chief
grief	conceit
deceive	receipt
eight	neigh
reign	

Rule #16

Below are listed some of the commonly misused homophones—words which sound alike but have different spellings and different meanings:

aural   *related to listening or to the ear*

oral   *spoken or related to the mouth*

council   *a group of elected or appointed officials or advisors*

counsel   *advice (noun) the act of giving advice (verb) or a group of attorneys (noun)*

idle   *not working, at a standstill*

idol   *an image of a deity*

principal   *the head of a school, "The principal is your pal."*

principle   *a basic truth or a rule of conduct, "He was a man of high principles."*

stationary   *unmoving, fixed*

stationery   *writing paper and envelopes*

waive   *to give up a right*

wave   *to make a back and forth motion, or the motions made by water*

SPELLING LIST

abridgment	absence	academically
accelerator	acceptance	accessible
accidentally	accommodate	accountant
accuracy	ached	acknowledgment
acquaintance	acquire	adjacent
advertisement	adviser	aerosol
aggravate	aisle	allergic
allotted	all right	almanac
a lot	amateur	analysis
anesthetic	anonymous	answered
anxious	apparently	cafeteria
caffeine	calculator	calendar
camouflage	campaign	cantaloupe
careless	Caribbean	carriage
castenet	catastrophe	caterpillar
cemetery	changeable	chassis
chlorine	chocolate	cocoa
coconut	cocoon	columnist
commissioner	committee	comparative
compatible	competence	complexion
concede	conceivable	conscience
conscientious	conscious	contemptible
controlled	corduroy	corroborate
counterfeit	coupon	courteous
criticize	cyclone	dealt
deceive	deodorant	descend
desperate	development	defendant
defense	deficient	delicatessen
disastrous	discipline	dissatisfied
divine	dominant	doughnut
dynamite	ecstasy	eerie
effervescent	efficiency	eighth

eke	elementary	eligible
embarrass	emperor	emphasize
endeavor	environment	epitaph
equipped	essentially	etiquette
exaggerate	exceed	excellence
excessive	exercise	exhilarated
extraordinary	extravagant	facility
fascinated	fatigued	February
feminine	fictitious	fiery
fluorescent	fluoride	foreign
forty	fourteen	funeral
gaiety	geyser	ghetto
glamorous	glamour	gnome
government	grammar	guarantee
guardian	gymnasium	handkerchief
harass	height	hereditary
hippopotamus	horizontal	hygiene
hymn	immaculate	immediately
incidentally	inconvenience	incredibly
independence	initiative	insistent
interference	interruption	irresistible
itinerary	jealous	jeopardy
jewelry	judgment	kayak
kidnapped	kindergarten	knowledgeable
laboratory	laminate	larynx
leisure	leotard	library
license	licorice	likable
likelihood	liquor	livelihood
loathsome	lovable	luxury
lynx	maintenance	manageable
maneuver	marriage	martyr
Massachusetts	mathematics	meadow
memento	metaphor	millionaire
miniature	Minnesota	miscellaneous

missile	Mississippi	misspell
moccasin	molasses	mosquitoes
municipal	murmured	mustache
naïve	neither	nickel
niece	ninety	ninth
no one	noticeable	notoriety
nuclear	nuisance	occasion
occur	occurrence	offered
omitted	opponent	pagan
pamphlet	parallel	parentheses
partridge	pasteurize	pastime
penicillin	perceive	permissible
perseverance	persistent	Pharaoh
pharmacist	phenomena	phonetic
phosphorous	picnicking	playwright
pneumonia	polyester	porous
possession	prairie	precede
preferable	preference	prejudice
prevalence	privilege	procedure
proceed	professor	pronunciation
propaganda	propeller	psychology
pursuit	query	questionnaire
racism	receipt	reciprocal
recognizable	recommend	reference
referred	refrigerator	regretful
regretted	rehearsal	reign
relevant	remembrance	reminisce
renown	restaurant	resume
rhinoceros	rhyme	rhythm
righteous	roommate	route
sacrilege	safety	sauerkraut
savvy	scenic	schedule
scholastic	scientific	scissors
seize	separate	several

severely	shriveled	sincerely
soccer	solar	souvenir
spatula	splendor	sponsor
strategy	strength	stubbornness
subtly	successful	suddenness
suede	sugar	sundae
superintendent	supersede	syllable
symphony	synonymous	tambourine
teammate	technique	temperamental
tragedy	transcend	trespass
trigonometry	truly	turquoise
twelfth	tycoon	typhoid
tyranny	ulcer	undoubtedly
unmistakable	unnecessary	vacuum
variety	versatile	vertical
veteran	weird	wholly
wintry	withhold	writ
writhe	yacht	yield

ANSWER KEY

UNIT ONE

LESSON ONE: NOUNS

EXERCISE A: (page 5)

1. A	2. A	3. C	4. A	5. C	6. C	7. C
8. A	9. C	10. C	11. C	12. A	13. A	14. A

EXERCISE B: (page 6)

1. P	2. C	3. C	4. P	5. P
6. C	7. C	8. P	9. C	10. C
11. P	12. P	13. P	14. C	15. C
16. C	17. P	18. P	19. C	20. P

Grammar Check: Making Nouns Possessive (page 8)

1. Jack's	2. children's	3. boys'
4. teachers'	5. professor's	6. Dick's; Sue's
7. babies'	8. women's	9. trees'
10. cat's		

LESSON TWO: VERBS

EXERCISE A: (page 11)

1. A	2. A	3. B	4. B	5. A	6. A	7. A	8. A
9. A	10. B	11. A	12. A	13. B	14. B	15. A	

EXERCISE B: (page 11)

1. T	2. I	3. T	4. T
5. T	6. T	7. I	8. T

LESSON THREE: SENTENCE PATTERNS

EXERCISE A: (page 15)

Answers will vary.

EXERCISE B: (page 18)

Answers will vary.

EXERCISE C: (page 16)

1. S-V-O	2. S-V	3. S-V-O
4. S-V	5. S-V-O	6. S-V-O
7. S-V		

Punctuation Check: Basic Sentence Punctuation (page 18)

1. Mrs. Murdstone was a pleasant woman with a nice smile. (D)
2. Do you like cookies and milk for breakfast? (IN)
3. Go to the bank and get some money so that we can go shopping. (IM)
4. People who live in glass houses should not throw stones. (D)
5. Help! There are five hundred people trapped in a burning theatre! (E)
6. Is Christmas your favorite day of the year? (IN)
7. I love the holidays better than any other time. (D)
8. Come to the telephone as quickly as possible. (IM)
9. Open the window. (IM)
10. Small children make a great deal of noise. (D)

EXERCISE B: (page 18)

Answers will vary.

Punctuation Check: Capital Letters (page 22)

"How are you?" called Mark to Jenny as she passed him on Oak Street. "I haven't seen you for a while."

"I'm doing fine," replied Jenny. "I'm taking French and accounting at Boston College, and I have not had time for anything except studying."

"Are you taking Principles of Accounting I or Advanced Accounting II?" asked Mark.

"Advanced Accounting II," replied Jenny. "I took Accounting I last year. What have you been doing?"

"I took a trip with my parents. We went to Paris, France and London, England. We got to see the Thames River and Buckingham Palace. We even caught a glimpse of Queen Elizabeth at the English Derby. The trip was great."

"It sounds as if you really enjoyed yourselves," said Jenny.

"We did. Next year we are going to the Holy Land. We will see all of the places of the Bible—the land where Jesus Christ walked and the places where He died and was resurrected. Then we will come back to the U.S. via a flight through Berlin, Germany."

"When will you be back?" asked Jenny.

"Not for a while. We have to spend some time in the East while my dad gets some work done. When Dad is ready, we will fly west, spend the night in Chicago, and then we will come home."

LESSON FOUR: ADJECTIVES
EXERCISE A: (page 27)
Answers will vary.

EXERCISE B: (page 28)
Answers will vary.

LESSON FIVE: ADVERBS
EXERCISE A: (page 30)

1. precisely
2. patiently
3. faithfully
4. eagerly
5. calmly
6. quietly
7. furiously
8. excitedly
9. well
10. smartly

EXERCISE B: (page 31)

1. inside   2. deeper   3. now   4. later

5. soon   6. quietly   7. badly   8. forward

9. Sometimes   10. recently

Grammar Check: Comparatives and Superlatives (page 33)

1. tastiest   2. muggier   3. better

4. worst   5. more enormous   6. hotter

7. sillier   8. smartest   9. braver

10. good, best   11. worst   12. better

13. best

Grammar Check: Recognizing Prepositions (page 35)

1. Near the door; with a broken arm

2. Inside the old house

3. beneath the trees; across the starry nighttime sky

4. Upon her arrival; from the doctor

5. Below the mountain; with the fragrance; of magnolias

6. at the station; within the hour

7. Until the man arrived; by the door

8. of the children; to bed

9. Throughout the school year; of punctuality

10. Along the road; of trees; with green, waxy leaves

LESSON SIX: SV-IO-O PATTERNS (page 36)

Answers will vary.

LESSON SEVEN: S-LV-N PATTERNS (page 39)

Answers will vary.

LESSON EIGHT: S-V-O-OC PATTERNS (page 40)

Answers will vary.

LESSON NINE: S-V-O-ADJ PATTERNS (page 43)

Answers will vary.

Grammar Check: Sentence Fragments and Run-on Sentences
EXERCISE A: (page 44)

1. <u>Birds are</u>; Sentence
2. Fragment
3. <u>Girls sell</u>; Sentence
4. Run-on sentence; My cousin could not swim. She took lessons at the YMCA.
5. Fragment
6. Run-on sentence; George promised to help his girlfriend with the party. He spent all day cleaning the garage.
7. Fragment
8. Run-on sentence; I want to become a better writer. I practice a little every day.
9. <u>we will be</u>; Sentence
10. Fragment
11. Run-on sentence; The work is too hard for one person. At least two people should be doing this job.
12. Fragment
13. Fragment
14. Fragment
15. Run-on sentence; The Fourth of July is a special holiday. It commemorates the birthday of our country.

EXERCISE B: (page 45)
The paragraph should read as follows:

When I was small, my brother and I spent many happy hours together climbing trees. When we were high in the boughs of the tree, we were certain that we could see the whole world. We could spend an entire afternoon enjoying the cool summer breeze through the branches. Then we heard Mother call us and tell us to come down because we were not allowed to climb trees.

Grammar Check: Regular Subject/Verb Agreement (page 47)

1. are	2. spend	3. have	4. is	5. like
6. were	7. need	8. search	9. are	10. are

LESSON TEN: TOPIC SENTENCES
EXERCISE A: (page 51)

1. **TOPIC SENTENCE:** *I always hated going to the dentist; I suppose that most people do.* **Sentence which does not belong**: I did, however, know a dentist, Dr. Roberts, who was a pretty nice fellow.

2. **TOPIC SENTENCE**: *The camel may be an odd creature, but it is perfectly suited for desert life.* All sentences belong.

3. **TOPIC SENTENCE**: *The emerging raisin is a delicious, healthful, and wonderfully versatile fruit.* All sentences belong.

4. **TOPIC SENTENCE**: *Small children have good imaginations.* All sentences belong.

5. **TOPIC SENTENCE**: *Exercise does not have to be unpleasant; it can be fun, safe, and extremely healthful.* **Sentence which does not belong**: In order to be really healthy, however, people must eat fresh fruits and vegetables and avoid fat and sugar.

EXERCISE B: (page 52)
Answers will vary.

EXERCISE C: (page 53)
Answers will vary.

EXERCISE D: (page 53)
Answers will vary.

UNIT TEST

Part I: Sentence Patterns (page 54)

1. S-V-O
2. S-V-IO-O
3. S-V-IO-O
4. S-V-0-ADJ
5. S-V-IO-O
6. S-V-O-OC
7. S-LV-N

Part II: Prepositions (page 54)

1. under the chair
2. with a cardboard box
3. Despite the many problems
4. in the park; amid the pines
5. to her desk
6. between Sarah and Mark; in the class photo
7. in the family home; on God's blessings
8. Throughout their lifetimes
9. Toward the end of the summer; up the river
10. Opposite the shore; with a silver fish; in its mouth

Part III: Capitalization and Punctuation (page 55)

"Do you want to go to the movies this afternoon?" asked Jeff.

"No, I'd rather go to the park," replied Joanne.

"Which park?" queried Jeff.

"Yellowstone, of course," returned Joanne

"What!" Jeff exclaimed. "Yellowstone is over five hundred miles away."

Part IV: Adjectives (page 55)

1. tall; <u>taller</u>
2. <u>best</u>
3. <u>worst</u>; long, irate, lazy
4. dewy, red
5. good

Part V: Adverbs (page 55)

1. extremely (adjective)
2. very (adjective)
3. critically (adverb)
4. fashionably (verb)
5. eagerly (verb)

UNIT TWO

LESSON ELEVEN: MASTERING DETAIL

EXERCISE A: (page 61)
Answers will vary.

EXERCISE B: (page 62)
Answers will vary.

Word Check: To, Two, Too (page 63)

1. To, two; too	2. to; to	3. two	4. too; to
5. To;to	6. to; too	7. to; two; too	

Grammar Check: Using Subject Pronouns (page 67)

1. he	2. she	3. he	4. He	5. he
6. she	7. he	8. She	9. He; she	10. he

Grammar Check: Using Object Pronouns

EXERCISE A: (page 68)

1. them	2. them	3. her	4. her;her	5. them
6. him	7. them	8. them	9. her	10. them

EXERCISE B: (page 69)

1. I	2. him	3. she	4. he	5. him
6. We	7. us	8. we	9. he	10. she

Word Check: Using Real and Really (page 70)

1. really	2. really	3. real	4. really	5. real
6. real	7. really	8. really	9. really	10. real

Grammar Check: Avoiding Shifts in Person (page 71)

An individual who wants to succeed in life should remain in school and earn a good education. Education really makes a difference because employers want to know about the grades of potential employees. Students should want their grades to be as high as possible because good grades will increase their chances of being hired. Studying is important for more than just career advancement, though. An individual who has a good education understands the world around him better. In addition, learning is interesting, and the more a person learns, the more interesting he finds his studies.

Grammar Check: Avoiding Shifts in Time (page 74)

One day I was out walking when I stopped to look at the flowers. Earlier in the day the weather had been hot, but by afternoon a nice breeze was blowing. I looked at my friend Sally and I said, "Isn't this a nice day?"

Sally replied, "Yes, it's the nicest day I have seen for a long time."

We stood there for a while, and then we turned around and walked back into the house.

LESSON TWELVE: DESCRIBING PEOPLE

EXERCISE A: (page 78)
Answers will vary.

EXERCISE B: (page 79)
Answers will vary.

Word Check: Commonly Misused Words (page 81)

1. They're	2. You're	3. Your
4. We're	5. there; their	6. were
7. were	8. You're; your	9. Their; there
10. We're	11. there	12. It's
13. its	14. It's; it's	

Grammar Check: Using Indefinite Pronouns (page 84)

1. likes	2. his	3. was	4. are
5. their	6. his	7. his	8. their
9. their	10. has		

Grammar Check: Using Reflexive Pronouns (page 85)

1. John, Linda and I went to the movies, and then we returned home.
2. C
3. Robert asked Mark and him to attend the party, but they did not want to come.
4. C
5. I went to work this morning and then to the market to get my groceries.
6. Pete and she are always going places together.
7. C
8. I needed the book, but you could have done without it.
9. Karen and I are going to judge the contest.
10. C

LESSON THIRTEEN: DESCRIBING PLACES

EXERCISE A: (page 90)

Answers will vary.

EXERCISE B: (page 90)
Answers will vary.

Word Check: A and An (page 91)

1. an; a	2. An; a	3. An; an	4. a; an	5. an
6. an; a	7. an	8. a	9. a	10. a

LESSON FOURTEEN: SIMILE, METAPHOR, AND CLICHÉS

EXERCISE A: (page 94)

1. S	2. M	3. M	4. M	5. S
6. S	7. M	8. S	9. M	10. S

EXERCISE B: (page 94)

1. Fact	2. Fact	3. M	4. M	5. Fact
6. M	7. Fact	8. M	9. M	10. M

EXERCISE C: (page 95)
Answers will vary.

Grammar Check: Coordinating Connectives (page 96)

Possible combinations are as follows:

1. Alfred worked hard at the market, and he had a second job at night.
2. The clouds hung low in the sky, and it looked as if it might rain.
3. The old car would not start, for it was out of gas.
4. The house seemed very gloomy, but many happy families had lived there.
5. Bill could have gone skiing for his vacation, or he could have gone hunting.
6. You may leave if you want to, but I need you to stay.
7. Irene spent a great deal of money on clothes, but she always complained that she had nothing to wear.
8. We like pizza better than hamburgers, so we ordered pizza.
9. I enjoy small dogs, and I also like cats.

Answers will vary.

Grammar Check: Using Subordinating Connectives
EXERCISE A: (page 98)
1. After the meal ended, we walked outside.
2. Because Jerry wanted a new car, he went to work.
3. Since all the houses on the block looked alike, it was difficult to tell them apart.
4. While the dog is sick, we will have to take special care of her.
5. Unless you go to the party, I will not attend.
6. If you need a ride to work, do not hesitate to call me.
7. Provided that the coffee is hot, I will have a cup.
8. No matter how I try, I never seem to make any headway.
9. Although you don't deserve it, I will give you a second chance.
10. Whenever you call me, I know that you want to borrow money.

EXERCISE B: (page 98)
1. We walked outside after the meal ended.
2. Jerry went to work because he wanted a new car.
3. It was difficult to tell them apart since all of the houses on the block looked alike.
4. We will have to take special care of the dog while she is sick.
5. I will not go to the party unless you attend.
6. Do not hesitate to call me if you need a ride to work.
7. I will have a cup provided that the coffee is hot.
8. I never seem to make any headway no matter how hard I try.
9. I will give you a second chance although you don't deserve it.
10. I know that you want to borrow money whenever you call me.

EXERCISE C: (page 99)
Answers will vary.

Grammar Check: Adverbial Connectives

EXERCISE A: (page 100)

1. The weather was very warm; therefore, we decided to take a walk.
2. Marta and John made very good law partners; in fact, they had a successful practice.
3. The doctor told me that I needed medication; furthermore, he wrote out a prescription.
4. Fran wanted to buy a new stereo; consequently, she took a part-time job.
5. Yellow on black is the easiest color combination to see; however, I hate the combination.
6. Christy's mother asked me to bake cookies for her party; moreover, she wanted me to serve them.
7. My children are the smartest in the family; indeed, they are straight A students.
8. I wanted to arrive at the meeting on time; therefore, I left the house early.
9. The house badly needs repainting; in fact, I bought a can of paint this weekend.
10. There is no space in the garage for a new car; nevertheless, my husband bought one.

EXERCISE B (page 100)

Answers will vary.

LESSON FIFTEEN: WRITING THAT ADDS DIMENSION

EXERCISE A: (page 108)

Answers will vary.

EXERCISE B: (page 108)

Answers will vary.

EXERCISE C: (page 108)

Answers will vary.

UNIT TEST

Part I: Coordinating Connectives (page 110)

1. Jeffrey has a pair of new tennis shoes, and he also has a new jacket.
2. You may do whatever you like, but if you help me, I would appreciate it.
3. We can spend the weekend at the lake, or we can spend it in the mountains.
4. We have acquired all the things we wanted, but we still are not satisfied.
5. The family experienced many hardships, but they survived them all.
6. Life is hard, but God is good.
7. We may have hot dogs, or we may have pizza.

Part II: Shifts in Time and Person (page 110)

Suggested revision:

I have really learned to appreciate my family because life is uncertain. I may wake up one morning and someone I love may be gone forever. I experienced this when my mother was in a nearly fatal accident two years ago. I left for work one morning, and she told me goodbye. Before I had gotten home that night, she had been rushed to the hospital and was having emergency surgery. As a result of that experience, I learned that I cannot take anything for granted.

Part III: Subject and Object Pronouns (page 110)

1. Between you and me, John is very incompetent.
2. Jane, Shirley and I are going to the movies.
3. C
4. We girls are going to the movies with Harry and him.
5. It is I at the door.
6. C
7. People need to know if he were the suspect or if the suspect were she.
8. Jeff is a better employee than he.
9. The person at the door was he.
10. C

Part IV: Indefinite Pronouns (page 111)

1. C
2. All of the people need to be treated with respect.
3. Some of the people are displeased with the decision.
4. Each of the teachers brought her own lunch.
5. All of the men are being held accountable for the actions of one.

Part V: Adverbial Connectives (page 111)

Suggested answers:

1. Because Bob and his employers could not agree on the money they owed him, they went to court.
2. The judge ruled that Bob was right, so he ordered the company to pay Bob $50,000.00.
3. Since the company appealed the judge's decision, Bob did not get any money until the appeal was decided.
4. When the appeals' court agreed with the judge's original ruling, they ordered the company to pay Bob immediately.
5. After Bob received all of his money, he continued to work for the company.

Part VI: Essay (page 112)

Answers will vary.

UNIT THREE

LESSON SIXTEEN: BASICS OF NARRATIVE WRITING

EXERCISE A: (page 119)

Answers will vary.

EXERCISE B: (page 119)

Answers will vary.

Word Check: Commonly Misused Words (page 121)

1. besides
2. beside
3. into
4. in
5. effect
6. effects
7. affect
8. Here
9. hear
10. here

Grammar Check: Using Relative Pronouns (page 122)

1. that
2. who
3. whose
4. who
5. whose
6. that
7. who
8. who

LESSON SEVENTEEN: WRITING SHORT STORIES

EXERCISE A: (page 130)

Answers will vary.

EXERCISE B: (page 130)

Answers will vary.

Grammar Check: Joining Clauses without Connectives (page 131)

1. Cinderella is a charming children's fairytale; it has been loved for centuries.
2. The story takes place in a kingdom far away; we are never told the specific location.
3. Cinderella is a beautiful girl; she has long blonde hair and huge blue eyes.
4. Her stepsisters are very cruel to her; they are jealous of her beauty.
5. Cinderella has no human friends; her only companions are mice who live in her house.
6. One day a fairy godmother appears to Cinderella; she gives her a chance to go to a ball.
7. At the ball, a prince sees her; he immediately falls in love.
8. Cinderella and the prince are married; they live happily ever after.

Word Check: Who and Whom (page 133)

1. Who
2. who
3. whom
4. whom
5. Whom
6. Who
7. Who
8. Who
9. Whom
10. Who

Grammar Check: Past Tense of Verbs (page 136)

1. walked	2. walked	3. took	4. spoken	5. burst
6. proven	7. written	8. taken	9. run	10. grown
11. spoken	12. wrote	13. knew	14. eat	15. ate
16. eaten	17. called	18. call		

Word Check: More Misused Words (page 139)

1. less	2. fewer	3. among	4. between	5. may
6. can	7. was	8. was	9. may	10. may not
11. among	12. less	13. fewer	14. was	15. were

Word Check: Using the Word Like (page 141)

1. Many people—my parents, for instance—are the children of immigrants.
2. Some of us, such as the Irish, came here many years ago.
3. People told my family for years that we looked as though we might be from Ireland.
4. C
5. My friend Sally looks like her mother, and her mother looks as if she might be Polish.
6. Other groups, such as the Russians, came to America at the turn of the century.
7. It is interesting to see pictures of family members from another country.
8. C
9. C
10. It is as though they are one big family from overseas.

UNIT TEST

Part I: Choosing the Correct Word (page 142)

1. Beside	2. besides	3. into	4. in
5. here	6. hear	7. effect	8. affected

Part II: Who and Whom (page 142)

1. The man who is the supervisor is my brother.
2. Whom are you going to call?
3. The flowers are for whom?
4. C
5. Whom do you trust?
6. Jack, whom you will meet in the morning, is very friendly.
7. C
8. Whom did the people elect as mayor?
9. C
10. C

Part III: Joining Sentences without Connectives (page 143)

1. The *Man in the Iron Mask* is a great book; I have read it several times.
2. Jeff is the lead basketball player; he is also the tallest person here.
3. Christy likes roses very much; this year she planted several rose bushes.
4. Rosie seems to have the perfect life; she has a great job and a wonderful husband.
5. He who laughs last laughs best; you should be laughing for the rest of your life.

Part IV: Using Words Properly (page 143)

1. fewer
2. may
3. can
4. C
5. C
6. as if
7. C
8. for instance

Part V: Essay (page 143)
Answers will vary.

UNIT FOUR

LESSON EIGHTEEN: USING CAUSE AND EFFECT

EXERCISE A: (page 148)

1. <u>If you develop the habit of gambling,</u> <u>you will eventually lose everything you own.</u>
2. <u>The baby began crying</u> when the ambulance sped screaming past the house.
3. <u>The frightened cat ran up the tree</u> when the snarling dog came charging from the barn.
4. <u>The cold wet wind hit the boys</u> <u>chilling them to the bone and causing them to catch cold.</u>
5. <u>Since the child was small and wiry, he could easily crawl through the large air conditioning ducts of the abandoned office building.</u>

EXERCISE B: (page 149)

Answers will vary.

Punctuation Check: Using Commas

EXERCISE A: (page 150)

1. To arrive at the airport before the flight, we had to leave in the morning.
2. My brother, to name one individual, was totally opposed to the new restrictions.
3. Howard Smith, on the other hand, liked every idea the company had.
4. To obtain all the information, we had to search through many reports.
5. In the end, however, we found what we needed.
6. During the entire process, I never lost faith.
7. Before the meeting ended, we were able to present our findings.
8. Delighted with the results, we left the meeting and returned to work.
9. Before the day was out, the changes we recommended had been approved.
10. In spite of the difficulties, we accomplished our goals.

EXERCISE B: (page 150)
Answers will vary.

Punctuation Check: Commas with Relative and Noun Clauses

EXERCISE A: (page 152)
1. C
2. His mother, who worked all day, used to ask me to babysit for him.
3. C
4. C
5. Spot would bite, even though Mrs. Marks said he would not.
6. He once bit a postal worker, who was trying to deliver a letter.
7. I was not afraid of Spot, though I knew that the other children in the neighborhood were.
8. My mother, who was frightened of dogs, used to ask me why I was not afraid.
9. C
10. Spot did everything that Eric, who was Mrs. Marks' older son, said.

EXERCISE B: (page 153)
Answers will vary.

LESSON NINETEEN: Cause and Effect Paragraphs
EXERCISE A: (page 156)
Answers will vary.

EXERCISE B (page 157)
Answers will vary.

Word Check: Expressions to Avoid (page 159)
1. Since he is my brother, I will give him a loan.
2. I agreed to go to the party because you were going to be there.
3. Since the dog likes me, I will let him stay.

4. I won't go to the doctor unless you agree to come with me.

5. At school, my teachers taught me how to write.

6. He is not going to medical school anyhow.

7. Somewhere around here is my brother's address.

8. The reason they wrote the letter is that they wanted to give us the new address.

9. Since this is my house, I can do what I like.

10. I will never speak to you again unless you apologize.

Punctuation Check: More Practice with Commas (page 160)

1. No Comma

2. There is no way we can finish by Tuesday, no matter what Mr. Davidson says.

3. No Comma

4. The door is locked, even though Jane says it is open.

5. No Comma

6. Before I won the championship, everyone told me I had no chance.

7. No Comma

8. No Comma

9. I have always supported your decisions, even when I did not agree with you.

10. If you marry for money, you will always be miserable.

LESSON TWENTY: COMPARISON AND CONTRAST (page 166)
Answers will vary.

LESSON TWENTY-ONE: EXPOSITORY PARAGRAPHS
EXERCISE A: (page 170)
Possible combinations as follows:

1. John wanted money for a new car; however, he refused to go to work.

2. Mark and Cindy were best friends; moreover, they spent all of their time together.

3. The little tree grew up in the scorching hot sun without any shade; consequently, in the summer it died.

4. Philip never studied in high school; in fact, he spent all of his time with his friends.

5. Philip never studied in high school; as a result, he failed every course.

6. Being President of the United States is a very demanding job; however, it is also very rewarding.

7. To get to my house, go to Scott Street and turn right; then, take a left at the stop light.

8. A knowledge of history can be very important; furthermore, it can help you in many professions.

9. Vicious dogs can be dangerous; consequently, they should be confined to their own yards.

10. People have a right to vote; moreover, they should take a greater part in government.

EXERCISE B: (page 171)
Answers will vary.

UNIT TEST

Part I: Punctuating with Connectives (page 172)

1. C

2. They need to know what is most important to them, and they must pursue the attainment of that goal.

3. Of course, there are many individuals who achieve enormous material success without a proper sense of values.

4. C

5. These people, however, eventually find that they have nothing except the material goods they have worked so hard to obtain.

6. Even the most beautiful, expensive items become meaningless when they become the focus of one's life.

7. On the other hand, individuals who place greater emphasis on serving God and helping other people than on achieving their own personal goals may not obtain a great level of material wealth, but they enjoy enormous spiritual, emotional and personal satisfaction.

8. C

Part II: Cause and Effect (page 172)
Answers will vary.

Part III: Comparison and Contrast (page 173)
Answers will vary.

Part IV: Expository Writing (page 173)
Answers will vary.

UNIT FIVE

LESSON TWENTY-TWO: PERSUASIVE WRITING
EXERCISE A: (page 180)
Answers will vary.

EXERCISE B: (page 180)
Answers will vary.

Grammar Check: Subject/Verb Agreement: Clauses (page 181)

1. have	2. are	3. has	4. are	5. has
6. is	7. are	8. are	9. is	10. have left

Grammar Check: Subject/Verb Agreement: Prepositional Phrases (page 182)

1. The <u>people</u> <u>near the river</u> are our neighbors.
2. The <u>girls</u> <u>beside the house</u> are sisters.
3. The <u>frogs</u> <u>of Green Lake</u> come out every spring.

4. The <u>bird</u> <u>above the trees</u> is an eagle.
5. The <u>canary</u> <u>with the golden feathers</u> sings beautifully.
6. The <u>friends</u> <u>across the room</u> belong to the same organization.
7. The <u>man</u> <u>inside the barn</u> has been working.
8. The two <u>girls</u> <u>in the office</u> are good friends.
9. The <u>grass</u> <u>outside the walls</u> has grown.
10. The <u>paintings</u> <u>opposite the mirror</u> were painted <u>by a famous artist</u>.

Grammar Check: Shifting from Active to Passive (page 184)

1. Jamie went to Milwaukee, found a job, and started a new life.
2. June won the election and took the oath of office.
3. The fishermen caught the fish, cleaned them, and took them to the market.
4. The trees grew big, spread out their leaves, and created a lovely shade for the animals.
5. The judge sentenced the prisoner who had pled guilty, and the authorities executed him.
6. The citizen's group fought city hall, voiced their disapproval of the bill, and defeated the legislation.
7. Mary Lee worked in the restaurant, struggled to keep her family alive, and realized her dream of having a better life.
8. The chickens lived in the yard, laid eggs for the family, and provided a chicken dinner at Christmas.
9. The committee drafted the proposal, drew up their recommendations, and submitted the complete document to the chairman.
10. Janie ran for office, managed her own campaign, and won the election.

Punctuation Check: Know When to Underline (page 186)

1. "The Knitting Done" is a chapter in <u>A Tale of Two Cities</u>.
2. Mrs. Morris was reading "How to be a Good Mother" in <u>Redbook</u>.
3. <u>Little House on the Prairie</u> and <u>Little House in the Big Woods</u> are books by Laura Ingalls.
4. <u>Daucus pucillus</u> is more commonly known as rattlesnake weed.

5. "Where I Lived and What I lived for" is a chapter from Henry David Thoreau's <u>Walden</u>.

6. <u>Haute couture</u> is the industry of leading women's fashion houses.

7. The <u>hors d' oeuvres</u> included stuffed mushrooms and shrimp cocktail.

8. To <u>corrupt</u> is to change from a sound to a putrid state.

9. <u>National Geographic</u> contains many interesting articles.

10. <u>Webster's Dictionary</u> is a useful resource book.

Grammar Check: Subject/Verb Agreement: Inverted Sentences
(page 187)

1. are	2. comes	3. Do	4. Has	5. lie
6. goes	7. was	8. am	9. is	10. was

Subject/Verb Agreement: Linking Verbs (page 189)

1. have become	2. have taken on	3. become	4. are	5. represents
6. has resulted	7. are	8. have become	9. are	10. are

UNIT TEST

Part I: Subject/Verb Agreement (page 190)

1. These are the best friends I ever had.

2. Here are the dishes you need for the party.

3. There are the kittens.

4. These are the things you asked me to bring.

5. C

6. The legislation requires that all paperwork be in on time.

Part II: Prepositional Phrases (page 190)

1. Down the hall, under the table

2. in glass houses

3. Over the river, through the woods, to grandmother's house

4. For the reasons, to your career

5. At the café, in the morning

Part III: Underlining (page 190)

1. <u>Good Housekeeping</u> contains the interesting column "Good Cooking."
2. I wanted to get some tips on growing Mr. Lincoln roses, so I bought the May issue of <u>Better Homes and Gardens</u> magazine.
3. <u>The Secret Sharer</u> is a riveting story by Joseph Conrad.
4. <u>Anne of Green Gables</u> and <u>Anne of the Island</u> are books by Canadian author Lucy Maude Montgomery.
5. When I was in school, I read <u>Jane Eyre</u> by Charlotte Bronte and <u>Ben Hur</u> by Lew Wallace.
6. <u>Junta</u> is the Spanish word for <u>council</u>.

Part IV: Persuasive Writing (page 191)
Answers will vary.

UNIT SIX

LESSON TWENTY-THREE: WRITING WITH QUOTATIONS
EXERCISE A: (page 199)

1. "Hang your coat in the hall closet," said Marsha.
2. "Careful! The floor is wet and slippery!" warned the janitor.
3. Mother snapped, "Do not run in the house!"
4. "Last night I shot a bear in my pajamas," quipped Groucho Marx. "How he got in my pajamas, I shall never know."
5. The little boy asked, "Is there any such thing as Santa Claus?"
6. The frightened child cried, "Where is my mommy?"
7. "You have to calm down," explained the police officer, "because I cannot understand you."
8. "You have been working for hours. You must be tired. Why don't you stop and rest?" suggested Mark.
9. "I think the dog ran away. I haven't seen him anywhere," announced Dad.
10. "Joey keeps hitting me, and I didn't do anything to him," sobbed the little boy.

11. "Take this money," exclaimed Uncle Joe, "and hide it where the police won't find it!"

12. "Do you ever wonder if there are aliens on other planets?" questioned the student.

13. "Stand there," ordered Mary, "and don't move until I tell you."

14. The waiter asked, "Are you ready to order?"

15. The circus trainer shouted, "Step right up and see the man-eating tiger!"

16. "If you are not ready to leave by now," called her impatient boyfriend, "you never will be!"

EXERCISE B: (page 200)

"Where have you been?" complained Jason. "The weather is getting really bad."

"Don't you think I know that!" retorted Mike. "I was the one getting rained on out there. Anyway, I was looking for my dog, Spot. I can't find him anywhere. I think the thunder scared him off."

"Do you think we should go out again and look for him?" asked Jason. "He could be killed in a storm like this."

"Sure, let's go," said Mike.

"Not so fast, you two!" called Mother from the other room. "The dog will find his own way home. You two sit down and eat your soup."

EXERCISE C: (page 201)
Answers will vary.

Grammar Check: Avoiding Double Negatives (page 202)
Suggested answers:

1. Diana could hardly finish her meal.

2. She would have gone with him, but she did not have anybody to take care of the baby.

3. Eric could scarcely get his horse up the hill.

4. James did not have any idea what was happening.

5. Mark could not get any more help from his parents after he told them a lie.
6. The dog would not drink any more water.
7. You should not buy any more flour until we use what we have.
8. David would not play with the older children anymore after the fight.
9. The cat does not come around anymore since I yelled at her.
10. I will not try anymore to get you to change your mind.

Punctuation Check: Using Commas for Special Information (page 204)

1. Yes, I plan to read Chapter 6, page 24 of the novel.
2. Mary, please get me the butter and sugar.
3. John is six feet, three inches tall and weighs two hundred twenty pounds, fourteen ounces.
4. I really appreciate everything you have done for me, Mr. Stevens.
5. You read the book, didn't you?
6. Margaret, not Johnny, is the head of the committee.
7. Jeannie plays with her doll, never with the truck.
8. Why, I had no idea that Missy and George were engaged.
9. Well, if you really wanted my help, you should have asked for it, Mark.
10. This place, Joan thought to herself, will never be suitable.

EXERCISE B: (page 205)
Answers will vary.

Punctuation Check: Commas in Dates and Addresses (page 206)

1. On June 1, 2011, I moved to my new home at 10500 Oak Avenue, New York, New York.
2. The wedding will take place Saturday, November 9, 2012.
3. Mrs. Myrtle wrote to me from her hotel at 25 South Street, London, England.
4. July 14, 1789, is a very important date in French history.
5. October 12, 1978, was the birth of their first child.

6. From Tuesday, September 10, through Sunday, September 14, the Greens will be having their open house.
7. The historic celebration took place Tuesday, June 9, 1952, through Thursday, June 11.
8. You may write to us at 1595 Brook Street, Philadelphia, Pennsylvania 10725.
9. On Monday, October 6, the neighbors arrived.
10. Friday, January 6, will be my last day with this company.

Punctuation Check: Numbers and Abbreviations (page 208)

1. The porcelain doll cost $125.65.
2. Jeanne went to work for AT&T after she finished school.
3. John's mother moved to 105 North Avenue, Washington D.C.
4. Six entries were chosen as the prize winners in the $100,000 drawing.
5. I rise at 6:00 A.M.
6. My parents did not arrive back in town until 11:00 P.M.
7. Mr. Jones and Dr. Johnson had an interesting conversation about St. Patrick.
8. The letter was signed "Harry Burton, Ph.D."
9. Mark Harris, Jr. will meet Mark Harris, Sr. for lunch on Friday.
10. In the year 1215 A.D., King John signed the Magna Carta.

LESSON TWENTY-FOUR: WRITING BUSINESS LETTERS (page 214)

Answers will vary for all exercises.

Grammar Check: Using Commas in a Series

EXERCISE A: (page 216)

1. Marissa likes to ski, hike, and play tennis.
2. Lisa's favorite foods are lasagna, spaghetti, and spumoni ice cream.
3. Lions, tigers, and bears live in the woods.
4. Glass, steel, and brick are common building materials.
5. Farmers, engineers, and miners all work outdoors at times.

6. Girls Scouts, Boy Scouts, and Little League are organizations that serve children.

7. Martha and Jane got up early, went to the store, bought groceries, and returned home.

8. Martin gathered the information, wrote up his findings, typed the report, and submitted it.

9. Great, round, marble arches graced the entrance to the ancient majestic city.

10. Slowly, precisely, and meticulously the carpenter cut the fine-grained oak slabs for the cabinets.

EXERCISE B: (page 216)
Answers will vary.

Grammar Check: Subject/Verb Agreement: Collective Nouns (page 219)

1. delivers	2. were	3. is	4. are	5. is
6. is	7. is	8. is	9. likes	10. has
11. were	12. is	13. has	14. is	15. is

LESSON TWENTY-FIVE: WRITING IN THE DIGITAL AGE (page 227)
Answers will vary for all exercises.

LESSON TWENTY-SIX: WRITING PERSONAL ESSAYS (page 233)
Answers will vary for all exercises.

Word Check: Using Good and Well/Bad and Badly (page 233)

1. bad	2. badly	3. badly; bad	4. well	5. badly
6. well	7. bad	8. good; well	9. bad; badly	10. well; good
11. bad; badly	12. well	13. well	14. bad	

Grammar Check: Using Sit/Set, Lie/Lay (page 236)

1. laying; lie	2. Set; sit	3. laid; lain	4. laid; lay	5. lie
6. setting	7. Lay	8. Sit	9. laid	10. lay

| 11. Set | 12. lay | 13. lain | 14. laid | 15. sat |
| 16. sitting | 17. lie | 18. laid | 19. laying | 20. lie |

Word Check: Other Commonly Misused Words (page 239)

1.	healthful	2.	mantle	3.	horde	4.	healthy
5.	complement	6.	complimented	7.	noisome	8.	enormity
9.	enormous	10.	mantel	11.	hoards	12.	discreet
13.	discrete	14.	appraise/apprise	15.	Realtor		

Grammar Check: Misplaced Modifiers (page 241)

1. Singing loudly, the taxi driver sped down the street.
2. Strolling down the street, we saw a statue.
3. My purse with my twenty dollars was found by the banker.
4. I found my Persian cat in the top of the tree.
5. From the top of the building, I saw a child fall.
6. The child, who was kicking and screaming, was taken away by his parent.
7. The rose, which had long thorns growing from it, tickled my nose.
8. My sister wore an elegant white dress to marry the policeman.
9. The candy, which was half-eaten, had been thrown into the wastebasket.
10. My neighbors, who were Italians, ran a very successful store.
11. She and her husband met at the bus stop and then went to have dinner.
12. Carrying my yogurt, I walked right into the glass door.
13. I went with my boyfriend to the movie which had a scary ending.
14. The dog, which had long gray and black hairs on its body, sat lazily in the grass.
15. People who live in glass houses should not throw stones.

LESSON TWENTY-SEVEN: AN ARGUMENTATIVE EDGE (page 247)
Answers will vary.

LESSON TWENTY-EIGHT: BOOK REPORTS (page 255)
Answers will vary.

LESSON TWENTY-NINE: EFFECTIVE TITLES (page 257)

1. C   2. B   3. A   4. B

UNIT TEST

(page 258)

There is no answer key for this final unit test.

INDEX

Available Titles from Frontier 2000 Media

Non Fiction:

No Regrets: How Homeschooling Earned me a Master's Degree at Age Sixteen

Writing for Today

Looking Backward: My Twenty-Five Years as a Homeschooling Mother

Adult Fiction:

The Fourth Kingdom

The Twelfth Juror

Children's Fiction:

Tales of Pig Isle

The McAloons:

> *A Horse Called Lightning*

> *A House of Clowns*

ABOUT THE AUTHOR

In 1986, Alexandra Swann graduated at fifteen years of age with a bachelor's degree in liberal arts from Brigham Young University. The following year, when she was sixteen, she received a master's degree in history from California State University. After graduation, she taught history, English as a second language, and basic writing skills for four years at El Paso Community College. In 1989, her book, *No Regrets: How Homeschooling Earned me a Master's Degree at Age Sixteen,* was published, in which she detailed her experiences with homeschooling. At eighteen, she was the keynote speaker for the Utah Home Education Association homeschooling convention, and from that time on she and her parents and siblings spoke at many homeschooling conferences around the U.S. In 1994, the Swann Family was featured in the CBS Television Series, *How'd They Do That?*

In 1998, Alexandra and her family started Frontier 2000 Mortgage and Loan, Inc., an El Paso, Texas-based mortgage company providing residential and commercial financing to companies and individuals in West Texas and Southern New Mexico. For over thirteen years Frontier 2000 has provided financing to hundreds of clients in El Paso, Houston, San Antonio, and throughout the state of New Mexico.

Alexandra served as the 2002 president of the El Paso Association of Mortgage Brokers and the 2005 president of the El Paso Women's Council of Builders. She was the 2003 Mortgage Broker of the Year for the El Paso Association of Mortgage Brokers and the 2005 Associate of the Year for the El Paso Association of Builders. She is the 2011 Chairperson of the Board for the El Paso Hispanic Chamber of Commerce.

In 2010, she and her mother, Joyce, started Frontier 2000 Media Group and re-released *No Regrets,* with a new foreword to the twentieth anniversary edition of the book updating readers on what her family is doing today. She is also co-author of *The Fourth Kingdom* and *The Twelfth Juror,* both published in 2010. *The Fourth Kingdom* was selected as one of four finalists in the *Christianity Today* 2011 Christian Book Awards for the Christian fiction category.

Made in the USA
Charleston, SC
30 December 2011